On Course with

Mike Weir

Insights and
Instruction from
a Left-Hander
on the PGA Tour

On Course with
Mike Weir

Insights and Instruction from a Left-Hander on the PGA Tour

Mike Weir

with Tim Campbell and Scott Morrison

McGraw-Hill Ryerson

Toronto Montréal Boston Burr Ridge, IL Dubuque, IA Madison, WI New York
San Francisco St. Louis Bangkok Bogotá Caracas Kuala Lumpur Lisbon London
Madrid Mexico City Milan New Delhi Santiago Seoul Singapore Sydney Taipei

McGraw-Hill
Ryerson Limited

A Subsidiary of The **McGraw·Hill** Companies

ISBN: 0-07-086363-6

4567890 TRI 09876543
Printed and bound in Canada.

Canadian Cataloguing in Publication Data

Weir, Mike
    On course with Mike Weir: insights and instruction from a left-hander on the
    PGA tour

Includes index.
ISBN 0-07-086363-6

1. Weir, Mike. 2. Golfers – Canada – Biography.
3. Golf. I. Campbell, Tim, 1957-   . II. Morrison, Scott. III. Title.

Publisher: **Joan Homewood**
Editorial Co-ordinator: **Catherine Leek**
Editor: **WORDworks/Bill Steinburg**
Production Co-ordinator: **Susanne Penny**
Interior Design: **Liz Harasymczuk**
Electronic Page Composition: **Liz Harasymczuk**
Cover Design: **Dianna Little**
Cover Photo: **Greig Reekie**

Photos: **Greig Reekie**
Family photos: **Courtesy of Rosalie and Rich Weir**

To my wife, Bricia, and my two daughters, Elle and Lili.
Thanks for always letting me know what's really important in life.

Foreword

I FIRST MET Mike Weir at the 1999 PGA Championship at the Medinah Country Club in Chicago and I immediately knew that we had a lot in common.

We are both young golfers who are working hard to make our mark in the golf world and have enjoyed a lot of success in the past year or so. Of course, there are some differences too. Mike plays on the wrong side of the golf ball and I don't. But since we have become friends, that difference has become a source of great fun.

During the AT&T Pebble Beach National Pro-Am, for example, Mike and I played a practice round together. For a little added challenge, I decided to play two par 3s as a lefty, to see how the other half lives. I bogeyed the first hole, but on the second hole – the famous No. 7 – I birdied. It was the first birdie I had ever made playing from the left side.

Another time, on a par 3 we drew a few other competitors into our little challenge. During the Skins Game at Predator Ridge Golf Resort in British Columbia's Okanagan Valley, Mike and fellow lefty Phil Mickelson played right-handed, while Fred Couples and I played from the left. It was great fun.

And fun is what we should all have playing golf.

I'm sure you can tell that both Mike and I love to play the game. And while we do enjoy our time on the course, we also spend a lot of time drilling and improving our shots. Mike's fellow lefties will find the instructional photos in this book unique and especially helpful. But whether you play from the right or left, I think you will find the insights of Mike and his coach, Mike Wilson, very helpful.

Most importantly, this book will intensify that burning desire to get out on the fairways and hit some balls.

Sincerely,
Sergio Garcia

Table of Contents

Acknowledgements

The authors would like to thank the following for their assistance and patience.

Angus Glen Golf Club
Kevin Thistle
Steve Bennett
Jim Weir
Rich Weir
Rosalie Weir
Craig Weir
Rob Gilroy
Dave McKinlay
Karl Tucker
Mike Wilson
Dr. Rich Gordin
Brennan Little
Greig Reekie
Bill Steinburg
Scott Kaiser
Cam Cole
Bob Weeks
Ken Fidlin
Kent Gilchrist
Leona Sawatzky
Catherine Leek

Introduction

A T THE AGE OF 13, there seemed to be only one way to get a satisfactory answer to the question that had invaded my thinking for months.

It made total sense. I had started playing golf, then started loving golf. That it began by swinging left-handed had brought me to what seemed like a very critical stage. The more I played around home in Bright's Grove, Ontario, the more I thought about it. Should I switch to become a right-handed golfer? It seemed to me there was only one person qualified to give the answer, the legendary Jack Nicklaus — which is perfectly logical, of course.

My very first teacher, Steve Bennett, our local pro, was a big Nicklaus disciple. Steve actually played an exhibition with Nicklaus when I was 10 years old and I still remember following those two men — equally big figures in my world as a kid — around the golf course that day. That's when I started to be taken by Jack Nicklaus. The fact that Steve loved and admired him so much had something to do with it, too.

I remember that I was getting good at golf and that I had already started thinking about being a pro golfer because it would be something great to do. There really weren't any great left-handed golfers out there other than maybe Ernie Gonzalez or Bob Charles, so it seemed to me that since Nicklaus was the greatest player ever, I should ask him what he thought about switching from playing left-handed to right-handed.

So I collected all the relevant details about my game and how I was improving. I included my handicap, some scores and some tournament results from that summer and I wrote him a letter. I didn't have his address, but I had read many a *Golf Digest* and knew he was a playing editor for the magazine, so that's where I sent my letter: "*Golf Digest*, attention: Jack Nicklaus."

An agonizing month went by. I still admit I was surprised the day the letter arrived, neatly typed on Nicklaus letterhead and signed by the Golden Bear himself.

His emphasis was to stick to my natural swing, that I should keep at it and work hard and stick to what I was doing. I was so excited.

He gave me a piece of advice that changed my outlook, that kept me going in the game of golf, that gave me some direction. My career has taken many different turns and paths — from being a mediocre junior player to working my way through to be a professional; from playing mini-tours, smaller tours and overseas tours to getting on the PGA Tour; and from struggling a little bit on Tour to improving to where I am now, through hard work.

My golf swing has also experienced many changes. Even as a professional, who was still trying to compete, some very fundamental changes were not only possible, they were very beneficial in the long run.

Now, I'm not Jack Nicklaus, but this is an opportunity for me to help some fellow left-handers who might be thinking about reassessing and changing their golf swings — working on your faults can change your game a lot.

Some of the people who were integral to the growth of my game are people you'll hear from in this book: my coach and teacher Mike Wilson, my sports psychologist Rich Gordin, and others. I owe them all a debt of gratitude and I'm sure you'll find them to be every bit as helpful as I have.

Jack Nicklaus

December 5, 1984

Dear Michael:

   I just wanted to thank you for writing and to wish you the best of luck in your hope of becoming a professional golfer. I have always believed that a left-handed player is better off sticking with his natural swing. In my new book, THE FULL SWING, I've devoted a whole section to tips for left-handed golfers, and it uses what I considered to be the key instructional photographs of my swing "flipped" to show them from a left-handed perspective.

   Best wishes for continued good golfing.

Sincerely,

Mr. Michael Weir
2646 Hamilton Road
Bright's Grove, Ontario
CANADA, NON 1C0

/md

1208 U. S. Hwy. #1, North Palm Beach, Florida 33408

CHAPTER 1

The Early Years

A Driven Youngster

MIKE WEIR is still often asked about "the letter," which is framed and hanging on a wall in his home, not far from the trophy he collected in September 1999 for his first PGA Tour win in the Air Canada Championship. While he bashfully acknowledges seeking advice from the legendary Jack Nicklaus, make no mistake, the two milestones of his career, the letter and the hardware, are connected by far more than some childish fantasy.

Indeed, the letter was from a hopeful youngster intent on making his mark, his vibrant dreams and his love for the game so strong that they often drove him close to suffering frost bite on his fingers. With snow all around, a young Mike Weir wasn't satisfied with the golf season Mother Nature provided in Bright's Grove, Ontario, a small community just north of Sarnia on the Canadian shores of Lake Huron.

Weir's urge was so strong to experience some form of golf action while the flapping of flagsticks and the unique aroma of freshly cut fairways were still months away, that it led him, at only 11 or 12, to happen upon a brilliant idea, one only a kid with an active imagination

It never mattered if it was a nice day. It was whenever I got the urge that I'd go off to smash balls into the lake. Maybe there was a golf tournament on TV and I'd get excited and grab my club.

and a "why-not?" sense of adventure could concoct.

Home, you see, was only a block from the edge of the lake and whether it was tournament golf on television or a conversation with friends that made him antsy to swing a club on any given day, Weir had discovered the perfect driving range just outside his door. A club or two in hand, and a bag of treasures accumulated over the previous summer (what else but treasures would you call those balls fished from the ponds of the nearby course?) in tow, Weir set off to indulge his hopes and dreams.

"I'd brush off some of the snow down to the grass and beat them out and watch them bounce down the ice on the lake. If I couldn't get right down to the grass, I'd just bring a tee and my driver and hit the balls onto the lake."

Christmas 1970: Mike, 6 months old, with older brother Craig to his right and oldest brother Jim to his left.

At one year of age, Mike enjoys toddling around the back yard in Sarnia, before the move to Bright's Grove.

Two-year-old Mike poses for the photographer.

Targets were easy to find — an ice pile here, a crack there, a snow drift a little further away. Weir was a smart junior, too. Not once did he ever try to retrieve his balls.

Of course, there is plenty of good weather in a typical golf season in the warmest parts of Ontario, plenty of days to play the real game. After classes at St. Michael's School or, later on, St. Clair High School were done for the day, or during the summer holidays, Weir spent more time at his second home than his first.

He was what is known as a golf course rat, which follows in the same fine tradition as the rink rat, opting to spend every possible waking moment at Huron Oaks, the community's public golf course and recreation center. It was easy for an enthusiastic kid to find

My Mom would always bring my dinner or lunch over there. I might be working a shift from 7 until 2 at the driving range. If I was playing late, it was dinner, too.

Mike started sports early. Kneeling in the first row, on the far left, 6-year-old Mike sits with the rest of his 1976 T-ball team.

a job working at the course's driving range. The pay was just right — "spending money," as his first boss, Huron Oaks head pro Steve Bennett recalled — though it almost seemed wrong to Weir to actually receive money to be at a golf course.

When he wasn't working the range and sometimes the bag room, the main activities in his young life were golf, tennis, golf, golf, swimming, golf, golf and golf. Meals were not a priority, either. Who had the time? But Weir's parents, Rich and Rosalie, knew better.

Weir was not unlike most kids. He loved sports, and lots of them. He played hockey in the winter, baseball in the summer, and he played well enough despite his size that he was a member of the traveling teams. There was always a game to play somewhere.

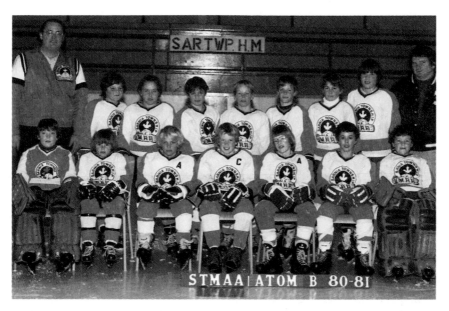

1980 Atom B, Sarnia's Travel Hockey Team: Second from the right in the first row, 10-year-old Mike was very aggressive on the ice. He liked to hit and often had parents in the stands yelling at him.

Baseball Team: Ten-year-old Mike is kneeling in the front row, second from the left. As a left-handed pitcher, he dominated hitters.

Working the Course

THE LURE of the golf course was undeniable and could not be ignored. However, satisfying that desire to play, even though the course was just three blocks from his Hamilton Road home, was not easy at first.

Being a natural left-handed swinger, like so many Canadian youngsters who grow up playing hockey, it was a very natural thought that a golf club could be swung the same way. You swing a baseball bat from the left side and you slap a hockey puck from the left side, so why not the same for golf?

Weir was the only left-handed swinger in his family, something his Dad knew from their occasional trips to the short nine-hole course at the Holiday Inn. A neighbor happened to have some old left-handed clubs and, at the age of nine, those Kroydon irons became Mike's first set. The next summer, however, Kroydons simply wouldn't do. Weir's Dad tried talking him into a set of new TNT irons, which he felt were within his Christmas/birthday budget for his youngest son, but the persistent young golfer had his eye on a used set of Wilson Staffs, one of the Cadillac brands of the day. Mike received his Staffs and they were high on his list of best friends for several years. Those clubs were evidence that golf had its hooks into Mike Weir.

It was good competition back then when they included me. And it was a great job. The pay — from what I remember, it was something like $3.25 (Cdn) an hour — it almost seemed wrong to actually receive money to be at a golf course doing what we were doing.

The head pro was in charge of monitoring play on the public course, his pro shop and bag room, of course, and also the driving and practice ranges. Each golf season, Bennett — who was the head pro at Huron Oaks between 1981 and 1992, as well as a family friend of the Weirs — hired local youngsters to clean clubs, fetch bags, put bags away, pick up balls on the driving range and do other odd jobs around the pro shop. Weir and his pack of friends, which included Dave McKinlay, Scott Hutchison, Dan Gates and Lee Cupick, were among the regulars in Bennett's employ.

Weir's buddies were all golf course rats and though they were all older by as many as four years, his peers were his rivals and his safe, secure pack of pals all rolled into one. At the beginning of their friendship, they merely tolerated the shrimpy Weir kid, but he became one of them before long.

Though they all entered various tournaments in the area on a regular basis, none were more important to the pack than the daily games at Huron Oaks, and the regular assortment of competitions around the small, undulating four-hole putting green outside the pro shop.

"At Huron Oaks, we really had a good time," Weir said. "We'd play golf, go for a swim, goof around and play tag in the pool, get cleaned up and go play golf again. There were tennis courts there, too. We just spent all our time at Huron Oaks in the summer. I spent most of my youth at that place and those guys, well, we're still close friends now."

Even some of the nicknames have stuck. One of Bennett's many endearing qualities was his ability to come up with nicknames. Weir was Geppetto. Gates was Gator. McKinlay, he was McGoo. Hutchison was Hutchy. Weir's older brother Jim was Julio. Weir and brother Craig have called each other Zeke for years. Neither is really sure why any more, but it might have had something to do with then-Detroit Pistons guard Isiah Thomas, whose nickname was Zeke. Mike, when he played basketball, was also a small point guard.

"They even called me Squale," Weir said. "They said it couldn't be Pasquale, because my Mom is Italian, my father's not, so I'm only half Italian."

Mike was also called Harry and still is by some of his friends. It had to do with his dark little mustache, which he had as a 12- or 13-year-old.

Also on staff for several years was Shelley Hocking, one of the inside pro shop workers, who often supervised the young staff. It was during one of the many visits to Huron Oaks to pick up his little brother that Jim Weir met his future wife. He also remembers some of the antics and work habits of the "munchkins," as he called them.

"Well, you have to remember they were just kids, that they loved to play golf, so it was the usual, not much working," Jim said. "But they were all very good players at a young age, all single digit [handicaps]."

Bennett remembers hiring Weir, "the kid from across the road," when he came calling one day to look for a job.

"Sure, I gave him the job for spending money," Bennett said. "Mike was strictly golf, golf, golf, it's all he wanted to do, but they all worked the range and bag room."

And kids, being kids, found their share of mischief.

"One of the first days I sent Mike out on the range, he sideswiped one of those green telephone connection boxes at the corner of the range," Bennett said. "Just swung around with the cart and whacked it with the tail end. He drove over our 100-yard sign on the range, too. Just flattened it."

Driving skills had plenty to do with another incident, which may have seemed equally unamusing at the time. Late one summer evening, a couple of the bag room pack buddies were joy-riding around the Huron Oaks parking lot on a cart, taking advantage of the wet pavement that day to slam on the brakes and spin the skidding carts 360 degrees.

"It was getting late, and we were yelling at them to come in but they wouldn't," Weir recalled. "So McKinlay and I jumped in a cart, he was driving and I was in the passenger seat, and went after them. We were chasing them down and they hit the brakes on a dry spot and they didn't spin and skid as much. They barely turned and we hit the brakes and slid right into them, just hammered the other cart and it caved in all along the side. We were worried about that damage, thinking about how much trouble we were going to get in when the flames started coming out of both sides of our cart. It had caught on fire, and the seat was on fire and it was all foam."

They ran inside to retrieve an extinguisher, which didn't help. An urgent call was made to the fire department, but by the time they arrived to put out the flames, the cart was ruined.

"It was about 80 yards out from the first tee, over there on the driveway," Weir said during a reminiscent visit to Huron Oaks. "It was all burned, with black smoke still coming out of it, so much that the neighbors started walking over to see what was going on."

Despite the cart mischief, Weir wasn't a troublemaker, though there was the time that Bennett fired him, albeit briefly. It was a rainy day and Bennett sensed the conditions could get worse. He decided it was time to clean up the range for the day. Weir thought they should wait until the weather blew over.

After some harping, Weir relented, but was unconvinced that he should actually have gone. He dawdled down one side of the range and back up the other, basically getting in another practice session, chipping balls back to the middle of the range. Bennett saw what happened and sent McKinlay out to send Weir home.

Mike, 16, with his first golf instructor, Steve Bennett. He still recognizes a lot of Mike's short game from those days at Huron Oaks.

"I took him off the work schedule for a week, mainly to teach him a lesson," Bennett said. "I guess you could say it was all part of his training, his growing up."

But Bennett, now the head pro at the nearby Sarnia Golf and Curling Club, relented a week later.

Bennett also remembers giving Weir a shot at working inside the pro shop, handling greens fees and sales when the head pro had scheduled a golf game one day. When he finished his round, he asked the young bag room convert how business went while he was out.

"He told me he sold a set of clubs and a bag," Bennett said. "Naturally, my first question was for how much? When he told me, well, all I can say is that I got those clubs on a clear-out so I made a few dollars on the sale, but that bag, oh my. It was a $135 bag and Michael sold it for $35.

"He told me he couldn't read my writing on the price tag. I asked him if it looked like a $35 golf bag and he didn't say much. I just told him it was a good thing he could golf because he didn't have much of a future in the golf shop."

A Young Temper

WEIR DIDN'T really want to be in the golf shop anyway. He wanted to play, and play he did, with a wide variety of family, friends and neighbors. Anyone who played with Weir noticed very quickly that he was feisty. He may have been young, but he had an intense, fierce competitive streak and it wasn't restricted to golf.

"It was especially there in hockey," recalled Mike's oldest brother, Jim, 10 years his senior. "He loved to hit. He was incredibly aggressive. I remember being at games when he played, where he'd hit some kid from the other team and look up in the stands to see if he was pleasing me or Dad, or whether he was making anybody mad. I can tell you that more than once he had other parents screaming at him.

"Dad always had the backyard rink at home. Craig and I used to strap the goalie equipment on him and fire shots at him. Got him in the teeth once or twice as I remember. I guess we kind of picked on him but that was the way it was in sports, all sports. We never let up on him at all and I think that's how he got some of his tenacity."

The aggressiveness was present in baseball, too. Weir was a good, hard-throwing left-handed pitcher in his tyke, peewee and bantam days and he used to dominate hitters. It was part of his personality, shaped in part by Jim, and middle brother Craig, who was eight years older.

Whatever the game, no matter how big or small, Mike hated to lose. Most of the time it wouldn't take him long to get over a blown baseball game, a poor night on the rink, or an unlucky day on the course. It just wouldn't happen in the first 10 minutes.

For instance, there was the 1984 junior club championship at Huron Oaks. Hutchison, then 18, and Weir had tied and were ordered back onto the course for a playoff. Their friends, of course, were front-row spectators for the showdown between the older, more-experienced Hutchison against the 14-year-old Weir.

Weir missed his chance to win with a short putt on the first extra hole and on the second, he was preparing to play in the fairway, taking some short practice swings. But he wasn't paying close enough attention to what he was doing and brushed his ball back about five yards. He was forced to accept the penalty, proceeded to lose the playoff on that hole and, needless to say, was stinging from the defeat.

I remember being very mad. It was a careless mistake to hit the ball while we were waiting for the group to clear on the second hole. I had missed a six-foot putt on the first playoff hole to win. To do that and then lose by one stroke, that was tough, especially because I was only 14 and those guys were about 18. It was such a chance to prove something. I can tell you I've never hit the ball by mistake like that again, so maybe it was a good lesson. It would have been OK to lose to a birdie, but to do something careless like I did was so infuriating. It wasn't anything about Scott. I remember walking in after the second playoff hole was over and talking about it.

"He was on fire," McKinlay said. "I remember how upset he was. We all kind of took him aside and told him not to be so upset, that things weren't that bad, but he wouldn't have any of it at the time. He said he was out to win and that's all there was to it. His competitive drive was unbelievable, even at 14. And he hasn't changed a bit."

"Yeah, that was Michael," said Bennett. "Michael was human, he was a kid and he'd blame something else. It was never his fault."

Weir's competitive nature has been an asset for a long time, but it used to come with a serious temper.

"Yeah, I had a temper, but I think it was an asset," he said. "In my competitive nature, I consider it an asset. I've never been one to think it's just a temper. It's better than being complacent. It's better to have some fire there, as opposed to being a person who gets down on themselves. If you have a temper, you can get rid of it quickly. If you hit a bad shot, you're mad and it's over with but you're not constantly talking to yourself, saying, 'I suck.' With me, it was the temper and then it was over."

But he could play golf, there was no doubt about that. To survive as the youngest member of the pack, in order to keep up with and be accepted by his older buddies, Weir simply learned to be better.

Early Development

WEIR NEVER shied away or backed down from a game with older friends or rivals. "I remember some of the older junior players, when I was 12 and

13, these guys were 16, 17, and that's a pretty big age difference when you're that age," Weir said. "They'd ask me to come along to play with them. Obviously, they were much better than me at that time. It gave me a lot of confidence to fight and battle to play with those guys and eventually beat them every once in a while."

Bennett laughed when he recalled the first reports of Weir's early proficiency on the course. "Yeah, the first question was always whether this kid knew how to count," he said.

I don't think they liked it too much but I had a competitive fire in me that I wanted to get out there. These guys were all three, four or five years older than me, working in the shop and they were good players, too. But they always included me in their games, the putting contests, and I think it made a big difference. It made me push harder to do well.

The first time Weir broke 40 for nine holes, shooting 39, he remembers proudly walking into the pro shop to announce his accomplishment. No one openly challenged his scorekeeping, but the next time Weir played, Bennett sent an assistant pro out to play with, and check up on, him.

"I shot 38 that time, so I think that's when they started believing me," Weir said.

Bennett became Weir's first teacher by default. This relentless kid was so determined to be a good player, his boss was the first and obvious choice for help in a very competitive region. Himself an adept short-game player, Bennett tried to stress its importance. "It's rewarding to watch how he's progressed, but I still see a lot in his short game that's similar to when he was a young kid," Bennett said. "He had a very strong mind for it at a young age."

It didn't take long for the signs of rapid development to show up in tournament play. In the summer of 1983, Weir joined his pals in several junior tournaments in the area. One such trip was to Seaforth, about a one-hour drive north of Bright's Grove. There, Weir went about his business, playing out ahead of most of his buddies. McKinlay, on a nearby hole, remembers seeing Weir over on the 18th green, putting from way above the hole.

"The hole was cut way down on the bottom right and he was all the way to the back of the green," McKinlay said. "I just remember thinking to myself when I saw him that, with his short game, he'd probably make that putt for something like 70."

Graduation: 1984 marked Mike's graduation from St. Michael's School into high school. Mike is seated third from the right.

When they finished playing, they found out that McKinlay's premonition had been correct. Weir made that last putt from about 40 feet, shot 70, and won the tournament by one stroke over a field that included 18-year-old juniors.

The remarkable thing about it was, at 13, Weir had only ever broken 80 once before, having shot a 79. He remembers that day at Seaforth, having made the turn at 36 and thinking to himself that he must concentrate on shooting 42 or better on the back to be able to post a career-best score. Of course, he was far better than 42, carding a 34 to win.

A week later in Goderich, another town on the shores of Lake Huron, at the Sunset Golf Club, Weir holed a 120-yard shot on his 17th hole for an eagle two. He then did the same thing on the final hole from about 80 yards away after chipping out of the trees, making a birdie to close with a round of 71. He won again by a single shot. His friends were all astonished and maybe a bit disappointed because they'd all been in contention, McKinlay at 73, Cupick at 72 and Hutchison at 74.

The spring in which Weir turned 14, he decided to give up baseball to clear more time for playing golf.

"I remember questioning him about why he wasn't going to play, about why he couldn't do both," Jim Weir said. "But I think he had started to have some success on the golf course and he enjoyed the individual sport more, maybe because he had a little more control over it. He was incredibly fierce in his decision, which with him is usually the understatement of the year."

> *It was where I worked. It was where I played. It was where I lived. It was what I dreamed.*

Mike began to spend even more time at Huron Oaks. While some friends didn't share his devotion to the game, for Weir golf was everything.

Looking Beyond Bright's Grove

ONE BREAK for Weir and his aspirations was that he lived very close to the United States. Michigan was just across the Bluewater Bridge from Sarnia and in order to seriously explore the possibility of golf in his future — thoughts that seemed more realistic after he won the Canadian Juvenile Championship for 14 to 16 year olds in Edmonton, Alberta, the previous summer — a decision was taken in early 1987 to play somewhere he could be noticed by American college coaches and recruiters.

High School Graduation: At 18, Mike graduated from St. Clair High School and looked south of the border, to the U.S., to continue his education and golf career.

At age 17, the decision to look south of the border paid off. Having qualified for the U.S. Junior in Vail, Colorado, Weir made it to the quarter-finals before being eliminated, and caught the eye of Brigham Young University coach Karl Tucker. A relationship was immediately struck; Weir was impressed with Tucker's approach and Tucker was "enamored," as he put it, with Weir's desire.

CHAPTER 2

The College Years

Getting Started at Brigham Young University

TUCKER, WHO is finishing his 33rd year as the golf coach at BYU, has vivid memories of his first introduction to Weir.

"I went to the tournament in Vail with two or three players in mind, and I don't mind telling you one of them was Phil Mickelson," Tucker said. "But I knew pursuing him would be a waste of my time. I had a few others in mind, but really, I was just looking around at some players when I started watching Mike.

"When he got through playing, I met him, and I was so enamored with him. He had something I knew I wanted and something which would be a big benefit to our golf team. We just hit it off and it was the beginning of a wonderful relationship.

"As a college coach, there are certain things you look at in players," Tucker said. "Some look a lot at scores. Some look at how long a player hits it. I look at a guy's overall attitude about what he wants out of life, out of his future, what he thinks the big obstacles are, and how hard he is willing to work.

"And don't forget, a non-Mormon kid coming to a Mormon school, that was not usual. But he told me he'd handle the school and not to worry about it. He liked my straightforwardness, I think, and I liked his dedication to how good he really wanted to be."

BYU is a church school and the atmosphere of the university is very religion-oriented. There is a little bit of Mormon doctrine in most classes. Sometimes it feels like you're not part of the whole deal because 98 per cent of the school is Mormon. They have church functions, their outings and things, and for me not to be included in those things ... that was what Coach was wondering about. The school part was not a problem. We had to take some religion classes, but it could be a variety of things. Outside of that, I'd say it was just handling the social aspect. Growing up in Canada, you like to have a beer here or there, but that's not part of the deal at BYU. There are no pubs on campus, though that didn't bother me. I told Coach not to worry about that because it wasn't what I was there for. I was there to get an education and to work hard on my golf game. I think he could see I wasn't going to "not fit in" and that I wouldn't embarrass the school in any way.

There were learning experiences in his new environment and in a different culture, but nothing of a magnitude that would cause alarm.

"We had a freshman dance, for everyone to get together to meet people, and I remember showing up in a pair of shorts and flip-flops on that hot summer night," Weir said. "But I had to be sent back to change because you weren't allowed to wear shorts and you had to have socks on.

"In intramural hockey, if you had a day's worth of scruff (on your face), you couldn't play. We'd run out to 7-11, get a couple of Bics and just dry shave. In my freshman year, it was just stuff like that you'd forget once in a while. Really, it wasn't much more than that. But it was part of the deal, because when you signed on, you signed a code of ethics, things you'd abide by, and I never really had a problem with that."

About half the players on the BYU golf team were not Mormon, including fellow Canadians Jason Thomas and Jeff Kraemer, but the team frequently socialized together regardless of religious background.

The fact that Weir was left-handed and Canadian was of no consequence to Tucker, either. In fact, he thinks being Canadian has occasionally proven to be an advantage.

Golf Trip: When he was 14, Mike and brothers Jim (left) and Craig (right) enjoyed a golf trip to Florida. Although Jim and Craig were older, Mike held his own and often presented quite a challenge to his older siblings.

"I consider Dick Zokol to be one of my great friends, Rick Gibson, too," Tucker said. "There are certain things about kids from Canada that seem to fit for us. We're here in the mountain country, with not that long a summer and certainly with a winter. If kids are willing to come to an atmosphere and a climate like this, they're willing to work hard to overcome things. It's been my experience that Canadian kids have something they want to prove and we, too, have something we want to prove."

"He invited me to BYU for a recruiting visit and I just loved that area," Weir said. "And there were so many other things going for the school. It had a great schedule, with a lot of good tournaments, and I was able to step in and play right away because some seniors had graduated. Plus there was a real Canadian connection there, guys like Jim Nelford, Richard Zokol, Brent Franklin and Rick Gibson had gone through there. Coach and I gelled right away and it sure was an easy decision after that."

The visit to Provo, Utah, was the final selling point and Weir, who was also recruited by Michigan State, Wright State, Marshall and Texas El Paso, signed up to begin his college career at BYU in the fall of 1988. It was

Brigham Young University Golf Team: A 1991 photograph
shows 21-year-old Mike in the center of the back row.
Mike found combining school with tournaments took some
forethought, but didn't find it that difficult.

a time to be enthused about college golf, Tucker said, because his newest
Canadian recruit had plenty to offer the team.

Even that summer before school began, Weir had, in a small way,
confirmed Tucker's read about the player he wanted at BYU. Weir won the
Ontario provincial junior championship.

Playing at College and at Home

WEIR CERTAINLY didn't waste much time showing Coach Tucker, and
many others, that he was serious about the game. Before starting his sophomore year he qualified for his first PGA Tour event, the 1989 Canadian
Open, through the 18-hole Monday qualifying round at Trafalgar Golf
and Country Club, west of Toronto. He shot 67, 4 under par, to join the
big names at Glen Abbey Golf Course for the Open.

During his sophomore year at BYU, Weir met his wife-to-be, Bricia.
They only realized it afterward, but they had lived that year in the same

apartment complex and met by chance at a small gathering arranged by Weir and Kraemer, his roommate and teammate, at their apartment.

One of Kraemer's friends turned out to be Bricia's roommate, who brought her along for the evening. That Weir and Bricia got together was an unexpected development because, Weir said, "I was actually on a date with another girl that night. I just remember spending more time with Bricia than the other girl I was on the date with."

Mike and Bricia continued to hit it off well, though golf occasionally threw them some curves. Once, in the early days of their relationship, Weir had stayed behind at her apartment to watch a golf tournament on her television while Bricia went to class.

As it always had, the sight of a golf course activated the need to swing, and Weir had a five-iron in his hands inside the apartment. A swing or two later, however, and there was trouble. He accidentally clipped the ceiling sprinkler from the fire-alarm system and the water started flowing.

"The whole thing was gutted by the time she got back from class," Weir said. "We had to pull out all the furniture, it fritzed her TV, and we had to take out all the carpet. It end up costing us about $1,500 [US]. I just couldn't get the water to stop. I stuck my hand up there but the little thing that spins around cut my hand. I was bleeding down my arm, trying to grab the garbage can and hold the thing up there to block the water. And the alarm was going off. I figured somebody would figure it out and just turn the thing off. This bucket was getting kind of full, getting heavy, so I let it go and ran all the way to the front desk of the apartment complex to tell them to shut the water off in that apartment on the first floor. By the time they shut it off, it didn't really matter. And there was rust in that water, because when it first came on, it left a big rust mark all the way around the walls. All of that for a five-iron."

When Bricia returned from class, Weir was busy trying to clean up the mess and was mopping up the floor.

"She thought I was just mopping the kitchen floor for her. But then she saw nothing in the living room, everything laying out in the snow. Needless to say, she was pretty upset."

With the firm understanding that golf clubs were no longer allowed indoors, Mike and Bricia were eventually married April 30, 1994, at St. Michael's Church in Bright's Grove, about a nine-iron from the first green at Huron Oaks.

Combining school with tournaments sometimes took some effort. There were usually four or five tournaments in the fall, and maybe nine tournaments in the spring leading up to the NCAAs. Some weeks, it was a tough balance, because we'd leave Wednesday night, play a practice round on Thursday, then start the tournament with 36 holes on Friday, play 18 more on Saturday, then come home. At BYU, we never played Sunday tournaments. It would be two days of school we missed, times 15 tournaments a year, but it wasn't that hard school-wise. I brought my books and, overall, I didn't think it was that difficult. One thing that helped was that early in the year, I got to set up my classes for earlier times in the day so I'd be done at one or two in the afternoon and have the afternoon to practice.

In 1990, before his junior year at college, he captured the first of two Ontario Amateur Championships, this one at Mississauga Golf and Country Club, upsetting Gary Cowan and Warren Sye, both former champions and dominant figures in Canadian amateur golf. The second Ontario Amateur win came in 1992.

Weir showed steady improvement at BYU and played well in his summers back home. However, his first of three college wins didn't come until his junior year, under trying circumstances, at a tournament in Monterey, Mexico, an event BYU had participated in for 20 years and had won several times.

On the final hole of the day, a par 4, Weir hit his drive into an area that had been very wet and also run over by a golf cart. His ball came to rest between some deep, muddy tire tracks and casual water was all around, but the rules official declined to grant Weir any relief. Tucker was furious.

"I told that gentleman that those were not the rules we played under and that I would take this above his head," Tucker said. "But Mike just came over and said, 'Don't worry, Coach, I'll just win it here anyway.' So he stood in that mud, hit his ball on the green and made the par and won the tournament by a shot.

"We never had to worry about counting his score. If you needed something special from him, he would always come up with it. You can usually tell that there's really something about the guys who have it. If Mike was having trouble, he'd work it out. I didn't always have the answers for him, but we could always find somebody who could help him and he worked out a lot of those problems."

BYU Golf Team: In the official portrait, Mike is in the back row, third from the right. Coach Tucker, on the far right, and Mike are still friends and live only 25 miles apart.

While BYU's golf teams were strong in Weir's junior and senior years, he was also making a mark for himself. He won a total of three college tournaments and was chosen as an All-American in his final year of eligibility. He was also named the Western Athletic Conference (WAC) player of the year.

One reason Weir and his teammates remained so sharp was Tucker's insistence that each member of the team qualify for his spot in tournament play. There was rarely an exception to the rule, even in Weir's senior year when he was selected as an All-American.

"One thing Coach did really well was that he made us qualify week in, week out," Weir said. "I think that

For me, college was always a great route because my career was always steady progress, not just a jump here and there. I think I needed those years of competition under my belt, playing against the likes of Mickelson, Herron and Stankowski week in and week out, improving at the college level. For me, it was definitely the route to go.

Playing on a team, those were some of the best days of my life. We got along really well. We played five guys as a team and they counted four scores every day. It was always exciting and you always knew you wanted to hang in there even if you were having a bad day because you never knew if one of the other guys might be having a worse day. It made you really fight and hang in until the end because you knew other guys were relying on you. Coach always made a point of focusing until the end every day. I kept seeing improvement throughout my senior year, which was a very important factor. I had 12 top 10s that season.

made a big difference in keeping us competitive all the time. It didn't matter if you had won a tournament most of the time. There were 16 guys and only five would travel. It was rare someone didn't have to qualify.

"Once I learned that lesson the hard way. In my sophomore year, we had a tournament scheduled at Fresno State and San Jose State, back-to-back, and my parents had planned a trip to watch me. They booked their flight out there but then I didn't qualify the week before. Coach knew they were coming, but I still didn't go. My parents went and watched the team, but I wasn't there. They were disappointed, I'm sure, but Coach always stuck to his word."

In Weir's days of college golf, there was never a shortage of competition in the tournaments, either. Phil Mickelson played at Arizona State about the same time. "We saw quite a bit of him," Weir said. "He was one of the best college players ever."

Certainly, Mickelson was one of the most accomplished. One of his feats was winning the PGA Tour's 1991 Tucson Open as an amateur, while still playing at Arizona State. Other rivals were Jim Furyk at the University of Arizona and Tim Herron at the University of New Mexico, a WAC-conference foe. Both have gone on to be PGA Tour winners.

"One guy I played against a lot was Paul Stankowski at Texas, El Paso [UTEP]," Weir said. "They were in our conference and we saw a lot of them. I had a good one with Paul in my sophomore year, his senior year, in the WAC [championship] at Coronado Country Club in El Paso and UTEP was ranked second in the country at the time. We took it to them real good, our team was way under par and we won the tournament. Paul and I had a good duel for the individual [championship]. I remember him chipping in on the ninth from a long way, in trouble, short of the green. I was up near the hole with what I thought was an easy up and down. I missed an eight-footer for par; it was a big two-shot swing there and he ended up beating me by two."

While at home for the summers of 1991 and 1992, Weir finished second in the Canadian Amateur Championship both years. The 1992 runner-up performance was on the heels of his second Ontario Amateur title, this one at St. Thomas Golf and Country Club. In early 1993, after he had become a pro, those results were recognized by *Score* magazine with an award as Canada's top amateur player for 1992.

As College Ends

AS DETERMINED as Weir was to become a good professional at the end of his college eligibility, Tucker was among the few who didn't think he was ready to make the jump.

"But I'll tell you this," Tucker said. "When he didn't make it in that first Q-school [PGA Tour Qualifying school], he went to play in Canada and in Asia and he did all the things you have to do. It took him five years to really get ready to play and I knew what he learned in those five years would put him in good stead. Absolutely, that was a good thing for him. And I don't think Mike has even scratched what he can do out on the Tour. He's just found out there's a field open and he's getting in shape for good things in the future.

For at least a year before I finished, it [turning pro] was what I thought of most. It was always in the back of my mind because it had been a dream for such a long time.

"I've had four or five of my guys make it through Q-school the first time and they didn't have the experience to stay. They lacked so much, they failed, and on the way back it's so hard to get back in."

As he built his game and his golf thought processes through four years of college, Weir's clear intent was to become a professional golfer.

He and Bricia decided to settle in Utah for reasons of convenience. When he finished school, he needed a place to play and practice and the facilities were available to him, especially during the critical time between

October and December when qualifying school was both a goal and a formidable obstacle.

"Really, I didn't know anywhere better," Weir said. "That's why we stayed, because of the facilities. Traveling was something I did a lot of, and it's pretty easy to fly [into Salt Lake City] from the west. Plus, I do like to ski."

"One of the things I really love about Mike is that he's made a commitment to his family," Tucker said. "I admire him so much for that. He's got all the tools, the strength of character. If he believed he could do something and it couldn't be done today, then fine; if it took a month or a year, then so be it, he would do it."

Tucker refers to Weir today as one of his "special friends." The two live only 25 miles apart south of Salt Lake City, Tucker in Orem and Weir, up the highway, in Draper.

CHAPTER 3

The Road to the PGA Tour

Earning a Canadian Tour Card

I N THE summer of 1992, Weir played an assortment of tournaments around his victory in the Ontario Amateur, all with an eye toward the fall when he would attempt the PGA Tour's qualifying school. When it came time to file his entry in September, however, Weir didn't realize the troubles that awaited.

All summer, he was gearing up to play for Canada at the World Amateur Golf Team Championship in Vancouver. What he hadn't realized was that, under the rules of amateur status, he was considered a professional as soon as his qualifying-school entry was accepted by the PGA Tour.

"I thought I was still able to play the World Am, since it was a month before the Q-school was to start," Weir said. "At the time, I'm not sure the story about that mix-up ever got told straight. I never realized that the professional status came right away, with the entry. It was only after I checked with the RCGA [Royal Canadian Golf Association] that I found out I was ineligible to play for Canada. It was very disappointing, but

CP PHOTO ARCHIVES (Sheryl Nadler)

I was committed to turning professional. It was what I really wanted to do and it was already too late to change that."

That qualifying school was the first of five unsuccessful attempts to obtain a PGA Tour card and without a tour to call home, Weir didn't play much golf that winter. He also had one more semester of school left to complete his Bachelor of Science degree in Recreation Management, which kept him busy to the end of the winter.

His professional career, however, began with an enthusiastic show of support back home, where Steve Bennett decided Weir needed more than just a handshake and good wishes to begin trying to make a living at golf. A fund-raising dinner was held in the gymnasium at the Huron Oaks community center. Bennett, along with Weir's family and friends, sold more than 100 tickets at $75 each and raised a cool $10,000 (Cdn).

"Steve knew I had no sponsors at the start because I was just out of college," Weir said. "I had no idea what he was doing at the beginning but it turned out to be this fantastic dinner. The support of the people in that area for their athletes is unbelievable."

Besides the dinner, giving him a job and being a lenient boss in earlier days, Bennett's role as a mentor was of ongoing importance. Once, when Weir was a developing junior of 16 or 17, Bennett gave him a set of newer Wilson Staffs as a Christmas gift.

"My old set was starting to show the wear and tear," Weir said. "Things like that are really something."

The money raised at the dinner not only helped Weir try the PGA Tour's qualifying school, but also assisted in his attempt to earn a Canadian Professional Golf Tour card in 1993. With the money, he was also able to play in Australia and Asia, where life was not always easy but thoughts of where he came from, and how, were.

"For some reason, I remember when I was playing in Australia that the money from that [dinner] helped me pay for my ticket down there and got me started," Weir said. "There have always been a lot of people along the way who have helped. The $10,000 that was raised the first time, I always felt that got me going, gave me the chance to get that experience internationally. It was important for a young guy to get his feet wet and get beat up a little bit. It makes you tougher. All those times make now that much sweeter."

There was one stage when he missed five straight cuts and he began to get into the Monday-qualifying rut.

"You had to Monday-qualify to play if you'd missed the cut the week before," he said. "I remember getting to Perth for one and I had a later tee time and I didn't have a caddy. I just used to throw the bag on a pull cart and go. When I got there, all the pull carts were out on the course. I had my big tour bag and nowhere to put my shoes because I had been dropped off by a cab. I threw my shoes in the side of the bag, and I carried my tour bag around, trying to qualify in probably 125-degree heat. I think I shot 73 in the wind and just made it. I just kept telling the other guys in my group, 'I might be a little behind here.'"

Sarnia really gets behind its athletes and I think that's why they pay so much attention to what I'm doing, because they have a vested interest. It gave me a good boost to get out there and work hard. For me, it makes me not only want to do well for myself but for those people who are behind me. Steve was a big part of that for sure.

Things were obviously a little more comfortable for Weir at home. He certainly never went without a caddy. Bricia carried the bag for two years on the Canadian Tour and during his second and third years on the Australasian Tour.

"She was a trooper," Weir laughed. "She carried that big tour bag all the time. I always told her we should use the small bag but she never wanted it. She wanted the big one. And in Perth, too, where it always seemed to be so hot. You'd go through 18 bottles of water and never have to go to the bathroom once."

The Canadian Tour was an easy choice for Weir in 1993 and he was eager to begin making his mark. The spring qualifying school was in Parksville, British Columbia, at Morningstar International Golf Course and it offered playing privileges for that year's Canadian Tour schedule to the top 35 players and ties.

In the days leading up to the competition though, Weir was hit by a severe flu bug that caused him to lose 10 pounds. He had struggled back to his feet by the start of the qualifying tournament and the worst seemed to be over, except on the morning of his first round. Weir forgot something in his hotel room and dashed back to get it, leaving his car running. When he returned, he discovered he had locked the keys in the running car.

The delay to get the door open cost him his warm-up time and he barely made his starting time, showing up on the first tee wearing running shoes. A friend saw him scrambling up to the tee and fetched his shoes out of the locker room. The hectic start, of course, left Weir susceptible to an unsettled day, but he overcame several early bogeys to get his round back to even par by the 18th. Nothing, it seemed, came easily in those early days of playing full-time golf.

"It was a huge, huge sense of satisfaction, just gutting it out because I wasn't feeling very good and wasn't playing all that well. I wasn't going along that well, even on the second day, and I was one over through 11 holes. It could have been very easy to miss the 36-hole cut, but I chipped in from a difficult spot on the 12th. Two holes later I holed a long bunker shot, then I birdied my last four holes and shot 66 out of nowhere."

That 66, along with a 70 and a 73 to finish, put Weir in a tie for sixth and he easily earned a membership card for the Canadian Tour. The spring school that year was won by Scott McCarron, now an accomplished member of the PGA Tour.

"I didn't have a lot of time to practice because I was so sick but I was able to put myself into position to win after three rounds and that's how I plan to approach all the events on the Canadian Tour in 1993," Weir told Canadian Tour communications director Rob Gilroy after securing his card.

Off to a Great Start

1993 and the Canadian Tour

The Canadian Tour began two weeks later at Victoria's Gorge Vale Golf Club, at the Payless Open. Weir's pro debut was mediocre. He made the cut, but his 53rd-place finish earned him $390.62 (Cdn). His second effort was less impressive. He suffered a quick exit with rounds of 76 and 74 at the B.C. Tel Open near Vancouver.

At the two Alberta stops that followed, Weir made another cut and finished tied for 24th at the Alberta Open, earning $977 (Cdn), but then missed the cut the next week at the Klondike Classic in Edmonton. In Winnipeg the following week at the Manitoba Open, Weir made some progress by shooting under par every day and finishing tied for 14th at 11 under, good for $1,562 (Cdn).

Two weeks later in mid-July, Weir's sixth tournament was the Tournament Players Championship at King Valley Golf Club, a long, difficult course north of Toronto. His scores through three days were 70-73-72 and he trailed Remi Bouchard and Steve Stricker by three strokes heading into the final round, which was being broadcast live on TSN, then Canada's only national sports television network.

Weir had only five players to pass for the lead, but playing in the fourth-to-last group of the day with Quebec's Jean-Louis Lamarre, Weir hadn't narrowed the lead when he made the turn to the tournament's final nine holes. It wasn't until the par 5 14th hole that Weir made his move. There, he hit his second-shot five-iron just six feet from the flagstick and made the eagle putt to jump to three under for the tournament.

On the next hole, however, Weir looked like he might give it all away as

I do remember not getting off to a good start on the Canadian Tour but I always believed I could muster some kind of game up and score with what I had. That's maybe when I started to realize I needed to change some things in my game but I knew I still needed to play well with what I had. I've always been able to score well with technique that wasn't that great, or that A-game. Those kinds of weeks — a bad tournament or a bad-luck tournament — never bother me. It's disappointing at the time, but they don't bother me in the long run. I've always been long-term goal-oriented.

he pushed his tee shot on the par 4 to the left and into the creek that bordered the hole. Forced to take a penalty stroke and a drop, he nailed a three-wood up to the green and left the ball 12 feet from the hole, then made a miracle par. The momentum carried over to the next hole, an uphill par 3, where Weir smacked his six-iron just right and knocked the ball two feet from the stick. The easy birdie carried him to 4 under for the week and into the lead.

From there, he managed pars at the final two holes and held on to win the TPC by a shot over Stricker, Bouchard and Richard Zokol, a fellow BYU alumnus. The national television audience watched Weir accept the $18,000 (Cdn) first-place check and when the Canadian Tour season wrapped up in September, he had earned a total of $25,555 (Cdn) and risen to eighth overall on the final Canadian Tour money list for 1993. He also won the Tour's rookie-of-the-year honor.

"I was a little jumpy on the back nine, but every time I had a difficult shot, I said 'trust it'" Weir said after his first pro victory.

After the tournament, there were golf writers who were so suitably impressed with Weir's showing that they predicted more would be heard from him. With early success and bold forecasts for a promising future, things seemed rosy indeed for the 23-year-old. But golf has a way of humbling players and so it was with Weir, who, with expectations high, spent the next three years barely keeping up.

That Fall, for instance, Weir had another Q-school disappointment, this one a difficult pill to swallow. At the second stage, Weir was involved in an eight-man playoff for one last spot in the coveted final stage. The spot was won by one of his rivals with a chip-in on the first playoff hole. Weir persevered, however, because the first alternates for the final stage would come from his site, Deerwood Golf Club in Kingwood, Texas. With three players remaining at the sixth playoff hole, a long par 3, Weir made a birdie to become the first alternate to the final stage in Palm Springs, California.

It was very disappointing, that second qualifying school. The officials told me that was the first time ever that at least one alternate didn't get in. The week probably cost me $3,000 (US), huge at the time, to not even play the final. On that drive back, about 13 hours, I was so disappointed that I didn't get a chance to get my card. I knew I was close, but I also knew I needed some work on my game. I just went to work to try to make myself better.

"It meant a pretty good shot at getting into the final in Palm Springs," Weir said. "I drove all the way down to Palm Springs, paid a caddie, played all the practice rounds to get ready. But everybody showed up. I waited until the last guy teed off and never got in."

The Next Two Years

In 1994, Weir fell to 15th on the Canadian Tour money list, hardly an alarming turn of events, but a tie for second at the Manitoba Open at Pine Ridge Golf Club typified his year. Weir led the tournament after three rounds and seemed a lock to win, but for no apparent reason on the back nine on Sunday, he started making bogeys — even cold-topping one off the tee and into the trees at the easy par-4 13th — and couldn't stop. By the time he reached the clubhouse, Scott Dunlap, another solid PGA Tour player today, had passed him for the top prize.

In 1995, there was a money rebound (to $43,933 (Cdn)) but no wins to show for his efforts — only more close calls, with eight top-10 and two runner-up finishes. The struggle carried into 1996, when Weir had three top-10 showings and dropped to 22nd spot on the money list with $20,715 (Cdn).

"I really hadn't been playing that well in 1996," Weir said. "I had discovered something the last day a few weeks before at the Canadian Masters and made a good score and I think that's what I carried over to the GVO [Greater Vancouver Open]."

Many may not have realized that earlier in the year Weir made a commitment to improve his game, one that would involve many trying days and weeks ahead. That spring, working with teaching pro Mike Wilson, serious changes were introduced into Weir's game.

1996: The First Big Change

THE REAL decision to seek changes in his golf swing actually occurred about 18 months earlier, Weir said.

"I remember being on the range at the Canadian Open, hitting balls beside Nick Price — I think in 1994 — and thinking to myself that if I wanted to get on Tour and not just get on, but play well, I'd have to beat a guy like Nick Price. Right now, there was not a chance of that," Weir said. "I always want to be positive, but every shot of his was streaking right at a flag with the right trajectory. And mine, well, they were mis-hit and sprayed all over the place. A light went on that day and I knew I'd need some changes."

The turning point was made on my own. I had been struggling through Q-school and missing. I had always known how to score but my ball-striking skills were never Tour quality. I just knew how to score, how to get it up and down and every once in a while I'd flash in a good score, maybe 67 and then a 77.

Weir made good on his determination that day and his and Price's paths would cross again several times.

Weir's transformation began with some experimenting on his own and plenty of reading in order to get some answers about the difference between Price's immaculate ball flight and his own inconsistencies.

"I found instruction books, trying to figure out the great players of the past and now, what fundamentals they all had in common," Weir said. "As George Knudson used to say, the golf swing is very individual, but there are some fundamentals that are the same for everybody."

There were no instant fixes for his golf swing, however, and results continued to be erratic. The maze of possibilities and options for change never deterred Weir, even as consistency continued to elude him. He said quitting was never an option.

"No, never," he said. "I don't know that word."

Wilson, a PGA teaching professional who is the director of instruction at Desert Willow Golf Resort in Palm Desert, California, had been teaching Brennan Little, Weir's longtime friend and current caddy. It was Little who suggested Weir meet Wilson for a "look-see" during a visit to the desert but it was what Wilson heard that first day that helped to forge their relationship.

"I immediately noticed the athleticism of his swing and especially the way his hips rotated through the ball," Wilson said. "It was quite unlike most of the players I had worked with in the past, but very reminiscent of many of the game's best players. I was also impressed by what Mike said at the outset of the lesson. He told me that he had the desire to become a world-class player. He also told me that he knew that his current swing was not performing to the standard that would hold up under the pressures of tournament golf at its highest level. He had a spectacular short game which would see him through the swing changes, but his swing needed modifications in order to repeat day after day."

It was in that spirit that Weir and Wilson began talking at their first meeting about what needed to be done, what the priorities and expectations would be and the commitment that was needed to achieve Weir's lofty goals. From that point, both knew that ahead were good days and bad, progress and retreats.

The week at the PGA Tour's 1996 Greater Vancouver Open at the Northview Golf and Country Club was among the early good signs. At the GVO, Weir came to the last hole, a long par 4 with an approach to the green over water, with a chance to force a playoff. He chose a six-iron for his approach but struck the ball at precisely the wrong moment.

"Up came a gust of wind and that ball went into the water," Weir said. "The thing was, I needed a birdie for a playoff, so I chose the club and took the chance at getting the ball close to the hole. When I won in 1999,

I came to the last hole with a two-shot lead and I took the extra club on that last hole because I didn't need to take the chance then."

But the disappointing, wet finish — tied for fifth when victory seemed so possible — did not produce the kind of anger normally expected from Weir.

"I felt then that I could play at this level," Weir remembered. "I had played close to a dozen [PGA Tour] events but I had never been close to contention. I was disappointed initially with how it finished, but heck, the next shot I had to make over that water on the last hole was even tougher because I dropped it into a sand divot. I got that up to 15 feet and made two putts for a six, which I was very happy about. I needed to make my shot on that last hole, and hey, at least I was there."

Even earlier in the year, Weir had shown himself something in terms of attitude, if not ability.

"Mostly, it was that every shot triggers the next shot," he said. "You never know when it's going to turn around in this game. In the German Open in 1996, I started off the tournament with a double-bogey and a bogey, but I shot 65 that day."

Clearly there was something gained from his experience, especially at the GVO. After another winter of playing a few tournaments in Asia, as he had since 1993, Weir returned for a fifth Canadian Tour season with new-found poise. Combined with the belief that some of his swing changes and concepts had started to become more comfortable, Weir had confided to Rob Gilroy of the Canadian Tour in the spring of 1997 that he had some new goals and that winning early was one of them.

1997: Gaining a Psychological Edge

IT HAPPENED in the second week at the B.C. Tel Pacific Open at Richmond, British Columbia's Mayfair Lakes Golf Course. Weir was the only player in the field to shoot in the 60s every day en route to a one-shot victory. This put to rest the talk that had dogged him for nearly four years, that he was an up-and-comer who should win again in Canada and hadn't. Fittingly, too, Weir won the tournament on the final hole, blasting a drive 322 yards and a second-shot seven-iron over water onto the green at the par 5. He two-putted from 25 feet to claim the victory.

In July, at the Canadian Masters at Heron Point Golf Links in Ancaster, Ontario, he ran away from the field with an 18-under-par 266, winning by eight shots. The top prize of $36,000 (Cdn) vaulted him to the top spot on the Canadian Tour money list. Carrying that momentum to the next event, the CPGA Championship at The Mandarin, just north of Toronto, Weir lost in a playoff to Guy Hill after both finished at 8 under.

In seven tournaments, Weir earned $80,698 (Cdn) and became the first Canadian in eight years to win the Canadian Tour's money title.

"He showed more confidence than he had in the previous couple of years," Gilroy said. "I think winning at Mayfair is what did it for him. Everyone had been reminding him of the GVO and this time he hit over water to win on the last hole. That set up his whole year. You could tell he was ready."

For me, not getting quite through the Q-school every fall, I wanted to have somebody to bounce some questions off. I kind of had a plan on the golf course that I wanted to be consistent with my thinking. I was trying to pinpoint why I'd have a bad round when my swing felt good, things like that. I had heard from my coach, Coach Tucker, that Rich was in the area, and Coach's father knew Rich's father through coaching. Rich had come from a golf background and in his position, as a sports psychologist at Utah State, dealt with a lot of Olympic athletes. He was a good guy to talk to. I was looking to cover all aspects of the game, all bases, and based on that, Rich was the guy I called.

It's very likely that another reason Weir was ready was a January 1997 telephone call to Dr. Rich Gordin, a sports psychologist on staff at Utah State University. Weir drove up to meet Gordin and, as with Wilson, there was a good connection.

"It was a wonderful conversation for a couple of hours," Gordin recalls of the first meeting in his office. "He was a delight. He answered many questions and we had a great visit. From there, we continued to work together."

That work included sorting out and prioritizing many things, both on-course and off.

"It was definitely more on-course things, like when it was time to play, being really ready to play," Weir said. "But in a small way, it was also things like the expectations of being Canadian and trying to get where I wanted to go. There was an added dimension there, especially when I was an amateur, hearing I might be the next great Canadian

CP PHOTO ARCHIVES (Sheryl Nadler)

Canadian Masters Win: Mike Weir looks at the George Knudson Memorial Trophy for winning the Canadian Masters golf tournament held at the Heron Point Golf Links in Ancaster, Ontario, July 27, 1997.

player. There was something there that had to be dealt with, and how would I deal with it? I had some ability in that way, but Rich was very helpful."

Weir's 1997 success in Canada opened other doors for PGA Tour events. He played in August at The Sprint International in Colorado and, in addition to the GVO and Canadian Open, he played in the B.C. Open in Endicott, New York.

The big test, though, came later that fall. After a decent finish playing for Canada at the World Cup of Golf, where he tied for 10th, Weir made his sixth trip to the PGA Tour's qualifying school, and for the first time advanced to the final stage. The preparation was always intense, and this year was no different.

"When you're playing any tournament, that's always in your mind, that Q-school is coming up and you have to get ready," Weir said.

Getting a PGA Tour Card

IT WAS at the first stage, however, that he came face-to-face for the first time with Jack Nicklaus, his boyhood golf idol, the man to whom he had written at the age of 13.

Weir was paired with Jack Nicklaus, Jr. at the Q-school's first stage in Indianapolis and during that round Jack and Barbara Nicklaus followed their son's progress on the course. During the round, Weir struck up a conversation with the elder Nicklaus and reminded him of the letter that had been sent and answered 14 years earlier.

"He said he didn't remember it but that, 'It was a good thing you stuck to left-handed,'" Weir recalled.

Later in the round on one of the par 5s, Jack Jr. pounded a three-wood from the fairway for his second shot, blasting his ball long and true and onto the green for a chance at an eagle. The impressive swing brought his father from the sidelines, asking to see the club with which the monster shot had been struck. "He took the club from Jackie and had a look at it and then he winked at me," Weir said. "He said, 'Can you believe this? It's an Arnold Palmer three-wood.' He was kind of laughing and we all had a big laugh that Jackie was using an Arnold Palmer club and not a Jack Nicklaus club."

In the first two stages of the qualifying tournament, the only prizes are trips to the next stage. At the third and final stage, the actual PGA Tour membership cards are finally on the table and this was Weir's first chance to claim one. "That year, with Bricia being pregnant for the first time, and it being so close to the final stage, then making it to the final stage for the very first time, I actually went into it with a different mindset — I felt lucky to be in the final stage for once," Weir said. "I actually felt relief, because that had always been my barrier, getting through the second stage."

He managed to stay close to the top group of players all week at the Grenelefe Golf and Tennis Resort. He was never worse than 72 in the first four days. After a fifth-round 71 that put him to 6 under par, he was on the bubble for his card heading into the final day.

In that last round, it came down to the late holes. On the 15th, Weir made a clutch par putt from about 10 feet. At the next hole, a par 3, he made a critical birdie, thanks to an impeccably struck four-iron stiff to the flag, that lifted him inside the line of successful qualifiers. When he had finished his round at 71, Weir knew he'd be close but he wasn't sure where he stood because a number of players were still grinding it out on the course behind him. At Q-school, there are no scoreboards out on the course and there's really no way to know where you stand unless you start counting up the numbers and names on the one main scoreboard.

"That last day, when I was right on the bubble, that could have been the most pressure-packed round I've ever played, by far," Weir said. "I was able to hit some unbelievable shots that day. I can't imagine anything as pressure-packed as that day."

The good, though not quite official, news came during a television interview.

"Donna Caponi [from The Golf Channel] came over and told me they had calculated that I was in, even with some groups to finish, and she asked me what it felt like to get a [PGA] Tour card for the very first time," said Weir, whose tears were visible in the post-round interview. "That's when the emotions hit me, because it was a dream come true, a dream I'd had since I was a kid first taking up the game."

I had finally done it. I was a card-carrying member of the PGA Tour for the first time. It had taken me six tries and knowing that I had finally done it was an amazing feeling. It's the happiest I've ever been about golf, even more so than winning the Air Canada [Championship], really. It sounds strange, that finishing 26th in a tournament was better than winning, but that's really the way it felt.

Weir's final round had put him into a tie for 26th place at 7-under, but the emotions had been magnified because Bricia was home in Draper, a week away from delivering their first child, daughter Elle.

"There were so many emotions going around me that week. That final day, I carried a picture of Bricia in my yardage book, just to remind me during the day of what was important."

Weir's graduation to the big tour meant two Canadians would be playing on the PGA Tour full-time in 1998, as Glen Hnatiuk had earned his card on the 1997 Nike Tour.

The Dream Realized: On the PGA Tour

The 1998 Season

Learning the Ropes

THE 1998 SEASON, Weir's rookie voyage on the PGA Tour, predictably had its ups and downs. There wasn't the opportunity to play every week in the early going because the new players from the qualifying school and the Nike Tour (now The Buy.com Tour) always had the lowest priority for entries. Weir played only five tournaments by the end of March and missed three cuts. In early April, he broke into the top 20 in New Orleans the week before the Masters, but from then until the end of May he missed four cuts in a row.

"It was a total adjustment during my first year on Tour," he said. "For one, I knew that I would be playing a lot at the end of the year and not early. And that was something new for me. Since I had been a pro, the most tournaments I had played in a year was maybe 15, you know, eight or nine on the Canadian Tour, a few in Australia and Asia and the odd one here or there. Basically, I was doubling my schedule. Finding out just how many tournaments I could play in a row and what my burn-out level was, those were new things for me to discover."

Playing new golf courses, most of them tougher than he had ever played, was one challenge, but figuring out how to get to these courses and where to stay for the week was also a new experience.

"Just finding a comfort level when you get to a new city, that was something," Weir said. "Being a new guy on Tour, it took some getting used to. There were a lot of new friends to make and life on the PGA Tour required a lot of adjustments.

"I wouldn't say the word is intimidating, but Tour life is more hectic. I think I spent too much time that year trying to see the golf courses as much as I possibly could. In that respect, I was trying to do too much but at the same time, I think I needed to do it and it paid off, especially in 1999. By then, I'd played most of the courses three or four times plus some practice rounds. It was a matter of being more comfortable and knowing how to play them."

Like any freshman, Weir learned the ropes. Contrary to what some say, life is not any more difficult on Tour for a left-handed player, though the fact that Weir hits the ball from the left side has created some unique circumstances as he has matured and become more well-known on Tour.

Left is Right

The lefties, for instance, have a common bond, Weir said.

"I don't know if I'd call it extra friendships but there's definitely a camaraderie out there," he said. "It's one of the neat things, that there are five other guys and you can see what kind of equipment they have. I'm using a Ping driver now because I tried Kevin Wentworth's two years ago in Tucson. I just went up to him and said, 'Let me have a swing with that big, ugly thing.' It felt so good, I had one in my bag the next week.

"It's tough sometimes, though, trying some equipment. Phil [Mickelson] is so tall and has big hands and his weighting is different. It's not much good for me. But with Kevin, Steve Flesch and Russ Cochran, their equipment is so close to mine that you can mess around with it. That's the kind of camaraderie I'm talking about."

That certain courses are more suitable for left-handers or right-handers is a grand fallacy, Weir insists. Closer to the truth is that golf courses tend to fit individual players. Sometimes, courses do favor a left-to-right shot, or a right-to-left flight, but there are both right-handed and left-handed players who shape the ball both ways. Some courses also fit a player's eye better than others, often for unknown reasons. Weir, for instance, said that Northview in Vancouver is one that sets up particularly well for him.

"But saying that there are courses for righties and lefties, that doesn't matter at all," he said. "It's not a lefty or righty thing. At St. Andrews a lot of people said there were so many left-to-right holes that it would be a good course for a lefty and, while that could be true for some lefties, for me it set up pretty well, but not that great. It's all a matter of how the courses suit the individual and his ball flight and his eye."

One issue that does concern left-handed players, Weir said, is equipment.

"When a new product comes out, usually it's right-handed first," he said. "A lot of times, it doesn't come out left-handed. There's a delay in the left-handed version most of the time. As a kid, that was difficult, to get the right equipment. Nowadays, you can pretty well get what you want. You just might have to wait a little for it."

As he learned the ins and outs of life on Tour in his rookie year, Weir did not bank bundles of cash. Neither was the 1998 season a complete flop. Though the learning curve was steep, steady progress was being made. In late August, for instance, Weir put together quality back-to-back weeks at The Sprint International in Colorado and at the Greater Vancouver Open, where he again tied for fifth, combining them to earn more than $86,000 (US). A few weeks later, after the Canadian Open, Weir added more than $48,000 (US) with a tie for seventh at the B.C. Open.

I knew the first year on the Tour was going to be the toughest. It was a new atmosphere, new players, new courses, and just feeling part of the whole PGA Tour. Having to go back (to Q-school), I had felt like my game was showing better signs in the later tournaments. I just went to work with Mike for a couple of hard weeks to hammer out some fundamentals and I went in with a great attitude. I was exempt right to the final stage, so I knew I just had to play one really good tournament. I knew — at least I felt — the second time around, I'd play much better.

The modest surge, however, was foiled by a late decline in sharpness and luck, as well as some fatigue, born of playing 11 consecutive weeks. It left Weir less than $10,000 (US) short of finishing in the top 125 on the money list and retaining his full PGA card for 1999. He earned just $7,959 (US) in his final four tournaments and his $218,967 (US) total was only good enough for 131st place.

Qualifying Again

Weir's 1998 earnings were hardly small but still meant another trip to qualifying school in California, this time at the PGA West and La Quinta Resorts. But this time he was better prepared. He had learned a lot. His progress with Wilson had drastically improved his game. Gordin was teaching him many things, including mental toughness. Most important, he had conquered the Q-school demons a year earlier and was confident he could do it again.

I've never been afraid to experiment with something that's going to make me score better and make me feel comfortable about the position of my golf club. A lot of people interpret the waggle to be very mechanical. Actually, it's designed to be very feel-oriented. I do drills to give my body the feeling of where the club is supposed to be. I'm a feel player, really.

As it turned out, this was the tournament in which Weir introduced his now-trademark pre-shot waggle, something he had found to be both comfortable and helpful in preparing him to execute a shot. The waggle is a half backswing, which allows him to see the plane of his swing.

It was not the first time he had tried something considered rather radical in the often staid world of golf. A few years earlier in Australia, Weir had made what's best described as a full-backswing waggle because he'd been having trouble getting his club on line. He took a full backswing, stopped it at the top and looked at it, then started over with his normal swing. It helped him through the day, though he didn't stick with it.

"I remember a few guys looking at me that day, wondering what I was doing," he said.

Warming up for the Q-school rounds, however, his new waggle invention seemed so comfortable, so right, he really didn't worry what others were thinking.

"I remember playing my practice rounds that week and going without the waggle, and not hitting it very well," Weir recalled. "After I played some holes with the waggle, I just told Mike that I was going to go with it because it felt so good, even though we'd just been using it on the range a lot as a drill.

"That 75 I remember shooting the first day was just a very bad putting round. It wasn't any indication my ball-striking was poor. That just tells you what a fine line there is in this game. I shot 75 and felt like I played, or at least was on the border of playing, really well."

It turned out to be a superb performance all that week in California. Even though it began with the frustrating 75, the putts began to fall in the second round, even a couple from 30 feet, to begin his charge toward the top. He finished that round with two eagles in the final three holes to shoot 65 and added 66 and 68 in Rounds 3 and 4.

On the final day, it was 64 — "as simple a round as you can imagine," Weir said — and it wrapped up the medallist's honor with a 24-under total. With that, Weir earned himself a prime card for the 1999 season.

When the new PGA Tour season started, there was an entirely different feel to it for Weir, who had now been around the circuit once. His confidence was as different as night and day. He also had much more control of his schedule.

And he had a new caddy. His former caddy, Dan Keogh, had carried his bag for two years. Keogh had married and taken a new job in the off-season and couldn't continue as Weir's partner. So, Weir contacted his old friend Brennan Little to tell him that the offer to carry the bag, issued informally some time earlier, was still open. Little was also a pro golfer, having played the Canadian Tour since 1995. They were the same age, turned pro at roughly the same time and were rivals in junior golf.

"When he won the Ontario Bantam [Championship], I think that's where I first met Brennan," Weir said. "We played against each other in college a little and we've been buddies for a long time. I think Brennan had decided in 1998 that it would be his last year on the Canadian Tour and I thought he'd be a great fit."

He knew my game and my personality and that's so important. Anybody can carry a bag and suggest a club to hit, but knowing the right thing to say at the right time, that's key.

The 1999 Season

More Learning Experiences

Weir missed cuts in three of his first five tournaments to start the 1999 season before finally starting to relax. A tie for 13th in Tucson at the end of February helped his confidence and in early April he burst into contention at the BellSouth Classic near Atlanta. Only a maddening final day, when he hit 16 of 18 greens but could manage only even-par 72, held him back but the final result, a tie for fifth and a check for $95,000 (US), was a sign of things to come.

"I had a good game plan," he said of the BellSouth Classic finish. "I followed it well. I didn't feel like this was a chance I had to blow to get the experience. I felt like I was going to win."

Two weeks after the U.S. Open, there was another strong performance. Weir, with 67s in the second and third rounds, moved into second place, four shots behind Tiger Woods at the Motorola Western Open heading to the final day.

As Woods and Weir battled through Sunday afternoon, the margin was cut to two at one point, but 70 wasn't good enough to win. Weir finished second, his best showing on Tour, and he cashed the largest check of his career, $270,000 (US).

The afternoon was also an up-close look at the whole Tiger Woods phenomenon. Woods is incredible on the golf course, especially when he gets into the lead. But being paired with him often means a day full of distractions, such as noisy, unsettled and constantly moving galleries tracking him around the course.

I don't really care who I'm paired with. With the kind of golf I play, I'm really into my own game. I don't want to sound blasé about it, I'm really not paying any attention to what the other guy's doing. I can't control what the other guy's doing.

That day at the Western Open represented one upward turn on Weir's learning curve on the PGA Tour. The British Open, two weeks later in July, provided another.

Weir had gone overseas a week early to try to qualify and was among only a few who made it through. His qualifying rounds were 71 and 66, rounds that were gutted out and fashioned mostly with a hot putter. At Carnoustie, nicknamed "Carnastie" by those who had experienced the

1999 US Open: After a day on the course at Pinehurst in North Carolina, Mike spends some time with brothers Craig (left) and Jim (right).

Family Time: Mike spends some time with his family at the US Open at Pinehurst in North Carolina. From left to right: Jim (brother), Rosalie (mother), Shelley (Jim's wife), Bricia, Mike with daughter Elle, Craig (brother), and Rich (father).

extreme rough and unfavorable weather in Scotland, Weir began his first Open Championship with a punishing score of 83.

Upset but undaunted, he returned the next day and got even. Gritting his teeth, Weir shot even-par 71 on Friday, a day on which the course had been so difficult that his 12-over total through two days was, incredibly, good enough to make the cut. His four-round total of 301, 17 over par, was not one of the best he had ever posted, but that 37th-place finish showed just how combative Weir can be.

"I know that was a huge step in finishing up the year the way I did," Weir said. "I was playing well at the Western Open but for some reason, when I went over to the British [Open], I just didn't feel comfortable with my golf swing. Carnoustie was an unbelievably difficult golf course. That first day, the wind was only blowing 35 miles per hour with big gusts. I shot 83. It's the highest I ever remember shooting. It was just brutally tough and I was so disappointed to get off to such a poor start."

Mike and Dino Ciccarelli's Charity Golf Classic at Huron Oaks: Stanley Cup was brought by Doug Armstrong (Assistant GM, Dallas Stars).

CP PHOTO ARCHIVES (Morry Gash)

PGA Championship: Mike, foreground, congratulates playing partner Tiger Woods after Woods won the 81st PGA Championship.

Conditions for the Friday round weren't much better, but Weir had channeled his disappointment into a sharp focus. "That day was a lot about me, feeling what I'm all about when I play golf, having a never-say-die attitude," Weir said. "It told me a lot about myself. Making that par putt on the 18th to make the cut by a shot, well, let's just say I was extremely happy the way I battled back. I just loved playing hard that day."

A month later, Weir was making headlines again, this time at another major championship, the PGA. And again he went toe-to-toe with Woods, shooting 68-68-69 in the first three days at Medinah Country Club. This time they began the final round tied for the lead, playing in the final pairing. And it seemed that the folks in Canada were paying attention.

Weir, unfortunately, lived a nightmare Sunday. He had detected a subtle change in the speed of the greens Saturday and hadn't felt like he'd adjusted very well. He was unsure about it early in his round Sunday and the uncertainty was visible. On the first four holes, Weir lipped out three putts that were just a shade too strong. His misery continued throughout the day. He wound up shooting 80, which dropped him into a tie for 10th.

"I tried to figure it out Saturday night a little bit but I still wasn't comfortable and the speeds were off. I just didn't have a very good feel. My touch wasn't good. So when you walk to the first tee Sunday and you already don't feel good about your putter starting the day, it's difficult to perform under those circumstances.

"On the other hand, I learned a lot from that round because I was so impatient with my putter. I tried to force, to make the putts and make something happen. Whenever you try to do anything, to force it, in the game of golf, it usually backfires. You've got to let things happen in golf. That's what I learned from that round."

Weir played the next week, in The International near Denver, but missed the cut. The following week, he simply went home to Draper to rest and reflect.

When the shot leaves the club and the putt leaves the putter, it's up to the mercy of the roll you put on it. It can hit a spike mark, it can lip out, it can hit an indentation. You can't control that and you have to learn to live with those kinds of things.

"I reflected more than anything about the PGA Championship," Weir said. "Then I just took it forward and made sure I had a positive attitude going into the Air Canada. I knew it [Northview in suburban Vancouver] was a course I liked."

Weir spent a quiet, uneventful week at home with Bricia and Elle and he made sure he did not dwell on his failure at the PGA.

"I don't lose sleep over that at all," he said. "Golf's a game where the only thing you can control is executing."

"You know, I hardly even practiced that week. I might have hit balls one or two days as I remember, but that's it. Most of the time, I was just at home."

The post-PGA weeks were an important time for Weir, according to Gordin, but there were no magical remedies or rebuilding of confidence that took place in dark offices or at practice ranges.

"We're only talking about a two-week time span here," Gordin recalled. "I flew back to Salt Lake City with Mike and Bricia and Elle after the PGA. We talked a little about it in the airport before we got on the plane in Chicago. Of course, Mike was very disappointed with how he finished in the PGA. If he hadn't been, I'd have been concerned.

"On the other hand, if you look at the entire week, a heck of a lot more went right than wrong. He had placed himself in a position to win the tournament by doing a lot of things well. We took a lot of lessons out of that tournament. It was the first time, too, that he had ever put himself in position to win a major on Sunday."

Those positives were Gordin's salve as he tried to reinforce the belief that losing the PGA was not the end of the world, or Weir's golf career. And Gordin was pleased with Weir's post-PGA attitude.

"He took a lot more away from it that was very positive than the distaste from the Sunday round," Gordin said. "One thing I'm very big on with anyone I work with is that you've got to take a lesson from every competitive round of golf, regardless of your performance, good or bad. The lesson for that week was staying patient and not trying to make things happen, and also not to change anything on Sunday in the final round. What got you there is what you have to stay with.

"Mike suspected these things himself. He's a bright, wonderful student of himself and the game. Sure, I point things out once in a while but it's better when the player points it out and I verify it."

Weir's missed cut the next week in Colorado was of little concern, Gordin said he remembers thinking.

"The week after the PGA . . . I think he was just tired, beat to shreds from Chicago," Gordin said. "I really didn't think too much about it that he missed the cut. He doesn't ever like to miss a cut but we didn't think we were in panic mode. We also took a few lessons from that.

"Then, he just went home and I went to Reno the next week for the tournament there. I was spending some time with another player I work with, Chris Perry. I don't think Mike and I talked more than once that whole week. He was at home resting, relaxing and he probably just took Elle to the zoo."

By Labor Day weekend, it seemed that the widespread disappointment over Weir's PGA finish had subsided, both in Weir and in Canadian golf fans ready for the show in Vancouver.

Plenty was learned, it would seem, in the three weeks following the final-day nightmare at Medinah. For it was three weeks later in Vancouver when a Canadian, Weir, won a PGA Tour event in Canada for the first time in 45 years.

The Big Win

"I did go up to Vancouver that week and I got there on Wednesday during the pro-am," Gordin said. "Mike was on the course and I went out to meet him and I walked around with him during his round for about nine holes. We talked and really, at this point, we had forgotten all about the previous weeks.

"This was a new tournament, and we were in Canada and my take was that there was a lot of attention being paid to Mike that week. Kevin [Albrecht, his agent] was there and the crowds were in high expectation of Mike after the PGA. In fact, he was being applauded and cheered, even when he went to the practice tee. Everybody was yelling to him from outside the ropes, yelling encouragement all during the tournament.

Because of all the extra hype, Rich and I decided to set up an approach to the entire week that would allow me the fewest distractions once the tournament began.

"At the start of the week, we talked about all the things he wanted to do that week, and we agreed that it was a good idea if he could get all his commitments to the press done early in the week," Gordin said. "Those are very important things and it was also important to allow him to concentrate on playing the golf tournament."

It seemed to pay off, though Weir began the Air Canada Championship inauspiciously with rounds of 68 and 70. On Saturday though, the tide quickly turned. Weir shot 64 to bolt into contention and was two shots behind leader Fred Funk, who was 13 under, by the end of the day. Between Weir and the lead were Carlos Franco and Phil Tataurangi at 12 under, one back of Funk and one ahead of Weir and Charles Raulerson.

Interest again soared in the young Canadian. As the clock ticked toward Sunday's tee time, Weir grasped tightly to the lesson recently learned at the PGA.

"The thing we did which was critical was to make a game plan on how to stay patient all week, Thursday to Sunday, to treat every day the same," Gordin remembered. "Even the shot on Thursday was just as important as the one on Sunday afternoon. This is how you win tournaments. I know he concentrated on making good putts and not letting lipped-out putts change his routine in any way. Finally on Saturday, putts started dropping. They did on Sunday, too."

I hit the eight-iron, landed it on the front of the green and the ball took two hops and began tracking toward the back hole location, looking perfectly on line from the time it landed. When it dropped into the cup, I heard the roar and tossed my iron up into the air.

His start on the first hole on a drizzly, dreary Sunday, however, was not good. Thanks to an unlucky bounce into a terrible lie, Weir made a bogey. But again, he showed his dogged determination and composed himself for the rest of the front nine at Northview.

"I could very easily have become impatient and tried to force things, but I held back, tried to be myself and let things happen and they sure did," Weir said.

"I know Sunday he had an early test and what allowed him to pass that test was what he did on Thursday and Friday," Gordin said. "You can't pass the test if you don't do your homework and Mike Weir has tremendous discipline and a lot of it kicked in that week."

The battle continued onto the back nine, when Weir struck the blow that his opponents could not overcome. He had driven into the left side of the fairway at the par-4 14th hole and had 164 yards remaining to the hole with a slight helping left-to-right wind.

"As I prepared to hit the shot, Brennan and I joked about how I hadn't holed out a single shot all week. He said to me, 'Why not this one?'

"I hit the eight-iron, landed it on the front of the green and the ball took two hops and began tracking toward the back hole location, looking perfectly on line from the time it landed. When it dropped into the cup, I heard the roar and tossed my iron up into the air."

After the tournament was finished, tournament organizers at Northview placed a plaque near the 14th tee commemorating the amazing shot, one that won't soon be forgotten.

The roar heard around Northview from the 14th also signified that Weir had vaulted into the lead and by the time he reached the 18th tee, he had a one-shot advantage over Funk. There, however, the leisurely pace of play caused a wait of almost 10 minutes, which probably seemed like half

CP PHOTO ARCHIVES (Chuck Stoody)

Greater Vancouver Open Win: Mike raises his trophy after winning the Air Canada Championship in Surrey, British Columbia, September 5, 1999, his first PGA Tour victory.

an hour to the players. Little talked to Weir about anything but the par 4 hole that had been his watery grave three years earlier on the final Sunday. They talked about the Blue Jays and wrestling until it was time to play.

A drive into the fairway left a familiar shot over the water to a flag close to the front. This time, Weir erred on the side of safety, selecting plenty of club and watching his ball go to the back of the green. His work was by no means finished, though, since he faced a tricky downhill putt of more than 40 feet.

The python of a putt rolled almost perfectly down the hill. It stopped inches from the hole and might have been his best stroke of the entire week. The gimme par putt ended his day at 64 and his tournament at 18 under, two shots better than Funk. Franco wound up two more back in third, while the group in fourth, six back, included Scott McCarron and Payne Stewart.

"This has worked out better than I thought," Weir said after the victory, which earned him a two-year exemption on the PGA Tour. "I want to keep making progress a little at a time. From where I came last year, maybe it was too early [at the PGA]. I knew I was close. I do have things to improve upon. Things happen for a reason sometimes and maybe there was a reason why it wasn't meant to be on Sunday at the PGA. I said I wouldn't dwell on it but that I wanted to be ready for the next time."

Weir became the first Canadian to win on Tour since Zokol did so at the 1992 Greater Milwaukee Open. A Canadian hadn't won a PGA Tour event on home soil since Pat Fletcher's victory at the 1954 Canadian Open. Weir also became only the sixth left-hander to win on the PGA Tour, joining Phil Mickelson, Bob Charles, Ernie Gonzalez, Sam Adams and Russ Cochran.

Attitude and preparation, it seems, paid off for Weir in a big way in Vancouver.

"I remember him calling me that Saturday night at home, just before he was getting ready to turn in," said Gordin, who had gone home to Utah Saturday morning to watch the rest of the tournament on television. "I remember telling him, 'Mike, you ought to sleep like a baby tonight.' He just laughed. What I meant was that he had done all the work and now all he had to do was to let the fruits of his labor pay off. He didn't have to do anything different. And one of the things I remember was during some of the comments he made to the press after he won. They asked him if he had a rough night on Saturday night and he said, 'No, I slept like a baby.'

"When you really look at it, the difference in the three tournaments [the PGA, the International, and the Air Canada championships] was very minimal. What it shows is that the mental training holds up. You don't always measure it in wins and losses. Sometimes you cannot win, when somebody else just plays well and wins, and you're still mentally tough. And some weeks, too, you can play not so well and still win."

The Mental Game

MENTAL TRAINING has become part of Weir's regular regimen, just as practice time on the range and a vigorous fitness training routine are incorporated into his schedule.

Gordin has spent plenty of time challenging Weir to discover more about himself and to help him find the best way to navigate through the high-pressure, high-stakes world of golf.

"He's just a good sounding board," Weir said. "He understands the game very well and, mentally, how delicate certain situations are. When certain situations arise, he's the guy I talk to about them, to try to correct things. Also, I just tell him what I think when I'm doing something well, to find out whether I'm on the right track."

Little, who has absolutely the best view of Weir's day-to-day abilities and progress, said his long-time friend has made some serious progress, not just with his swing, but with his thinking.

"I see that his attitude is getting better," Little said. "He can still be impatient at times but he's way better. He expects a lot of himself. And sure, there are times where it's tough to be patient, like for three days at the British Open at St. Andrew's when you're not making any putts. Then, you just have to hang in there but it's not the easiest thing to do.

"Rich has certainly helped him become more patient and positive and focused. Mike concentrates on the right things. I guess you could say in the past, he could lose his focus a little bit but Rich has been great. He's helped him learn how to have a better attitude on the course, to be more level, less upset, not too high or too low."

Gordin's guidance has also helped Weir find a workable approach to everything that surrounds his game.

"He's helped me become organized with my golf game and how I approach the game," Weir said. "He makes me very regimented and very organized. Simplified is a good word, too."

That simplification has been a godsend in many ways. Gordin said that eliminating distractions is one way to build toward that mental toughness.

"Mike works very hard at eliminating those distractions, and there are a lot of them on the Tour," Gordin said. "By distractions, we're not putting them in any negative context. They are what they are, and they're real."

PGA Tour distractions include, but aren't limited to, sponsors, the media, family and friends and things like tournament ticket needs, the weather, the course and what your particular history at any given tournament might be, the fans, other players and the practice range.

"The range is often one of the biggest distractions," Gordin said. "You need to know if you're there to do some work or to be social, and you want to do both because the PGA Tour is a small world. Mike, by the way, is a very popular guy and that's because he's genuine, so you know on the range, he'll be interacting with any number of people."

Distractions simply can't be ignored all the time, so dealing with them is a required skill.

"My general rule is that you can't control what happens to you, but you can control how you respond to what's happened to you," Gordin said. "What I try to get athletes to work on is to stay in the area of control rather than the area of concern.

"That's how you go for maximum control. It's like getting the interviews out of the way early in the week. And where Mike has the most control is inside the ropes. I always tell him that's your office, that's your sanctuary. Get your business done in there. You can take care of that other kind of business when you're outside the ropes.

"In psychology, we call it compartmentalizing. It means that whatever you're doing, do it 100 per cent."

Gordin has urged Weir to adopt the same strategy when he's with his family or friends.

"Another aside to that area is to try to have fun with the media, too," Gordin added. "You've got to talk to them, even when you shoot 76. You've still got to answer the questions, just like when you shoot 65, so you might as well try to enjoy it. I know it's not always easy but it's worth the effort."

I've always been long-term goal-oriented, and not even about next week or even next year. I just want to keep making my game better and not put a time limit on it. I want to keep working at it like I always have. I don't have any expectations that way. It's much easier to play that way than putting on too many expectations. However, my goals are higher now than they were a couple of years ago. Then, it was just keeping a [PGA Tour] card. My confidence level is better now. If my swing keeps getting better, and I keep working at it, those things will take care of themselves.

For all the methods and discussions and lessons that have gone on between Weir and Gordin, don't for a second think that it was an eight-week or 18-month course to learn better mental approaches. It's ongoing work, just like Weir's work to improve his swing.

"He'll be working on this for the rest of his career, which is OK," Gordin said. "It's how you get better. I always remember that quote from [UCLA basketball coach] John Wooden, who won 10 national championships. He said: 'It's what you learn after you know it all that counts.'

"Another quote I love, and I'm not sure who it's from, is: 'The road to success is constantly under construction.' You're always working on getting better. Mike works on his game, his conditioning and his mental game. That's just what champions do. If you reach a goal, you've got to go for something else, you've got to set a higher one to keep you reaching."

Weir's experience in gunning for PGA Tour and major championship titles has helped him develop a very useful mindset, especially when the pressure goes up on the golf course on Saturdays and Sundays.

"When I'm in contention, it usually means my focus is very good," Weir said. "And that means that if I have 143 yards to the hole, all I'm thinking is that I want to land it maybe 135 yards and have it skip up to the hole and stop. I honestly say I never think about the situation I'm in. I just go out and try to execute the next shot and try to make the best of the next shot.

"Brennan keeps me aware of where we might be in the tournament and maybe if we need to have a little change of plan coming in. Really, I try to keep it pretty boring."

Weir also said that his focus does not make him more relaxed.

"I'm not really relaxed when I'm in contention for a golf tournament," he said. "It's hard work, your mind's alive and active, your body is active. You just have to execute. If you watch me play, I'm very methodical. The whole deal for me is that I go through the routine and hit the shot."

After Weir's whirlwind week at the GVO, a pay day of $450,000 (US) and all the flag-waving he initiated, there wasn't any rest. And as the game of golf often has it, things did not take care of themselves the following week across the country at the Canadian Open at Glen Abbey Golf Club in Oakville, Ontario. Glen Abbey is a course Weir had not mastered. Though he was toasted and saluted at every turn by friends, family and fans at the national open, he was also scrutinized closely and only managed rounds of 73 and 74, suffering his eighth straight missed cut in an Open at the Abbey.

That didn't stop his momentum though, it just interrupted it. The next time out, at the B.C. Open, Weir finished in a tie for 10th, and three weeks later at the Michelob Championship in Kingsmill, Virginia, his three rounds of 74-63-68 put him into the lead heading into the final day. Sunday's 70 was disappointing in that it left him one shot out of the playoff between Notah Begay III and Tom Byrum, but it was Weir's seventh top-10 finish of his break-through season.

One other event in 1999 was both significant and prominent in Weir's overall success. At the Export 'A' Skins Game in June at Quebec's Mont-Tremblant, Weir beat three well-known rivals to earn $210,000 (Cdn). Though the made-for-TV event is mostly about entertainment, Weir, David Duval, Fred Couples and John Daly were not in it just for the fun.

"For me, the Skins Game was important because at the time, David was the best player in the world. [He'd already won four tournaments that season.] And everybody knows the kind of golf Freddy and John can play, so the way I played against them gave me a lot of confidence," Weir said.

"To outplay those guys, even though it wasn't a medal-play tournament, it was still competitive. I just remember making key putts at key times, and there's no more pressure than that putt I had for $150,000 (Cdn) at the 16th hole. All those things you put in your memory bank. I know Freddy has done that. He wasn't very happy about being shut out."

Outgunning his high-profile rivals at the Export 'A' Skins game, Weir also touched off some flag-waving in his golf-mad home country. He said he's only too happy to have the pro-Canada faction urging him on, something that also happens with surprising frequency during the regular PGA Tour season.

CP PHOTO ARCHIVES (Ryan Remiorz)

Skin's Victory: Mike Weir lifts his trophy after winning the Export "A" Skins game at Le Diable course in Mt. Tremblant, Quebec, June 29, 1999. Weir won $210,000 (Cdn).

"All the time, I do feel like I'm carrying [the flag]," Weir said. "It's fantastic. Not many people get the support I get, no matter what the city or region. There are easterners on their winter holidays in Florida when we're there. There are people from Vancouver and the west in California when we're down there.

"Even at the [2000] British Open at St. Andrews, it seemed like there were hundreds and hundreds of Canadians there. It's so fantastic, that everybody's shouting where they're from. The other players, they may get that kind of thing one time a year or so, when they're in their home town or area. For me, it seems like it's every week."

"Sometimes, they're yelling about lefties, too," Little added. "Sometimes they're yelling that they're from Nova Scotia or somewhere else. At the British Open, there was even this guy who was yelling he was from Petrolia [not far from Bright's Grove]. You just wouldn't believe how many Canadians there are everywhere we go."

When the cheering was finished in 1999 and his official earnings were tallied — including $83,000 (US) for a 26th-place tie at The Tour Championship in Houston in late October, a somber week in the wake of Payne Stewart's death — Weir had won $1,491,139 (US) in 30 tournaments and finished 23rd on the Tour's money list.

It was a watershed year for Weir in many ways. His learning curve turned into a performance curve. His sense of belonging on the PGA Tour was more than evident. And Canadian golf fans and their serious hopes had finally found a PGA Tour player able to meet their expectations.

Most of Weir's progress, though, was in separating his real job — getting the ball into the hole as efficiently as possible — from the onslaught of daily variables that are only magnified for a PGA Tour player.

"It is an interesting job because you get paid for how you play," Weir said. "There's nothing guaranteed in this game. And next week, it doesn't matter how you played last week. That's what I really like about the game. You don't have to rely on anybody else. It's just you. Sure you have people who kind of help you along, but it's really about you and how much you put into it."

The difficult part for Weir, he said, was not the work on his golf game. It was the time away from his young family.

"I try to have them out on the road with me as much as possible, but that's not always easy," he said. "But this is a great way to make a living and it is something I love to do. I couldn't think of anything better."

For the first time in eight years, the end-of-season numbers also didn't add up to a trip to the Q-school.

The PGA Tour had started to feel a lot more like home for Weir. He had certainly made many friends, and kept a lot of old ones. Many of his

I didn't think about not being at Q-school until the final stage was on and I was watching it on The Golf Channel. I remembered that only a year ago, I was right there. The game is so difficult that it made me want to work harder to not have to go back there again. It's so difficult to get through that. It also made me feel how lucky I was; that even though it's been a long journey, the hard work was finally starting to pay off. I guess watching it on TV and not having to be there made me feel like I had arrived out here, that I felt part of the PGA Tour. Before, I wasn't sure if I belonged.

tournament practice rounds were played with buddies like Craig Barlow, Dudley Hart or Notah Begay III, and some of his new friends and rivals like Davis Love III, Fred Couples and Justin Leonard.

The PGA Tour, however, is rarely a party place, especially for family men like Weir. Travel, tight schedules and long pro-am days are all factors that make free or leisure time a valuable commodity.

"In general, the Tour is a pretty tight-knit community, [PGA] Tour guys, their wives and families," Weir said. "Everybody kind of knows and supports what everybody else is doing out there. And for the most part, everybody gets along well with everybody else.

"With a young family, when I get my game done and my practice in, then I'm out of there. I like to get back to have time with my daughters and my wife, to have dinner with them. It's difficult to get out with other couples, or to get the kids and meet at a certain time. That's why we eat in a lot."

The beginning of the 2000 golf season marked several changes for Weir. For starters, he'd already begun to find himself in tournament pairings with more accomplished players. And as a tournament winner himself, a trip to the season-opening Mercedes Championships was earned. His place on the money list and in the world golf rankings also brought his first invitation to the Masters, the first time in seven years a Canadian was invited to participate. It was the only major Weir hadn't played in and by the time he reached the hallowed grounds of Augusta National in the first week of April, he'd already recorded four more top-10 finishes.

Anticipation was a double-edged sword during that first week of April 2000. Weir nearly didn't make it to Augusta and his first Masters when Bricia was a few days overdue with their second child, but on the Monday before the tournament, daughter Lili was finally born.

Weir was the last competitor to arrive, but his first Masters was well worth the wait — he began the final round tied for fifth before slipping to 78 on Sunday. Weir's short game served him well during his first tournament taste at Augusta, where local knowledge and being on the proper side of the hole are not merely suggestions, but survival tips.

CHAPTER 5

The New Millennium

Building Momentum

CP PHOTO ARCHIVES (Denis Doyle)

I N THE FOUR weeks that followed the 2000 Masters, Weir chose to take a break in his schedule in order to be home with Bricia, Elle and new daughter Lili. He didn't return to Tour life until mid-May in Texas. It was a disappointing resumption at the Byron Nelson Classic but in the two ensuing weeks, the break appeared to have paid off with a tie for eighth at the Colonial in Ft. Worth, Texas, and a fourth at Nicklaus' Memorial Tournament in Dublin, Ohio. At the second major of the year, the United States Open at Pebble Beach, Weir struggled through his first three days but authored an excellent 69 on the final day to move into a tie for 16th.

The British Open at St. Andrew's in July gave him similar fits, this time mostly with his putter, and a tie for 52nd was all his game could yield that week. A tie for 30th place at the PGA Championship at Valhalla Golf Club in Kentucky kicked off a stretch of four straight weeks, which included his title defence at the Air Canada Championship.

Weir's razor sharpness seemed to be just beyond reach during those weeks. His scores were unimpressive and momentum and consistency were elusive. He did

71

break one old jinx though by shooting 69 on the second day of the Bell Canadian Open at Glen Abbey to make his first-ever cut in the national open in 10 attempts. A three-week break followed, primarily for more family time and also to be a part of best friend Dave McKinlay's wedding back in Bright's Grove.

Weir returned to the PGA Tour at the Michelob Championship in early October with a bang. "Taking extended breaks has been pretty good for me," Weir said. "It tends to refresh the mind because playing tournament after tournament is a grind. That's given me some more insight into myself, too, about being game-ready."

I want to be really ready and prepared to play, otherwise I'd rather be taking the week off. In the last six weeks of the season, I felt like I was ready every week.

Weir began Sunday's round at the Michelob four shots off the lead, but rallied on the back nine with four birdies in the last five holes, including an 18-footer on the final green, to shoot 64. David Toms, behind him on the course, also finished at 13-under-par and the two went back to the 18th tee for a playoff. Toms found the fairway with his tee shot on the par-4 hole, while Weir's ball hit in the fairway, but about five yards left of where he was aiming and it skipped hard to the left. The ball ended up in a deep lie just a foot into the rough and on a slight downslope. His shot to the elevated green came up short, as did his pitch, leading to a bogey five. Toms' par 4 won the hole and the playoff.

"It was disappointing not to win but I looked at it as a great thing," Weir said. "I had just taken three weeks off, hadn't played at all and I was a little rusty to start the week. But I hung in there and Saturday I could feel it start to come around. I had a strong finish to shoot even par [71] that day and I had a strong feeling things were about to click for me on Sunday. No matter the result of that playoff, I actually felt like the week gave me some momentum."

The Presidents Cup

AS IN 1999, the signs of an imminent breakthrough were present. On the strength of his victory at the 1999 Air Canada Championship and six more top-10 finishes earlier in the 2000 season, Weir qualified for the

Presidents Cup 2000: Mike and Bricia at the Presidents Cup at the Robert Trent Jones Golf Club in Virginia. Weir was partnered with Nick Price (in background) against Americans Phil Mickelson and David Duval in one match.

International team for The Presidents Cup in October at the Robert Trent Jones Golf Club in Gainesville, Virginia.

With 12 of the best non-European players pitted against 12 of the best U.S.-born stars of the PGA Tour, the high-profile team competition began lightly enough at the opening ceremonies when International team captain Peter Thomson referred to Weir as the team mascot during player introductions.

It was meant — and taken — in good fun, helping Weir with his sense of belonging on the star-studded team that included Price, Norman, Elkington, Masters winner Vijay Singh and Ernie Els, among others. "What a feeling, hearing the Canadian anthem at the opening ceremonies, and it was first, too," Weir said. "I felt a great sense of pride representing Canada in a competition like that. It was a big goal of mine all year and there was a lot of emotion that night, being there for myself and for Canada and knowing that plenty of Canadian people were excited about it, too."

The competition was strictly team-oriented, including several functions for the players, their wives and children, before the serious golf began. There were team dinners each night at the nearby Marriott Hotel, each side in its separate special quarters, a private place to socialize and unwind from the day's play, practices and ceremonies.

When The Presidents Cup was played in Australia in 1998, the International side scored a decisive victory. Such a result meant there was plenty to talk about before the 2000 matches began that Thursday.

"Anticipation was the word," Weir said. "There wasn't much tension between the sides because almost all of the players knew each other well."

The Presidents Cup lacked the outright gamesmanship of 1999's storied Ryder Cup and was also without the glares, the animosity, the unruly crowds and pockets of contempt that marred that now infamous event. Of course, that didn't stop the Internationals from trying to stir the pot in a good-natured way on the opening day.

Egged on by his teammates and possibly by a few beverages all around, an at-first-shy Michael Campbell of New Zealand was persuaded during Wednesday night's pre-event meetings to show off a version of a *haka* dance, the traditional pre-game ritual of the world-famous All Blacks national rugby team from New Zealand. It took some convincing, but Campbell agreed to do a *haka* dance right in front of the American side just before the first match was to begin on Thursday.

"The cameras were ready and I think somebody from our side tipped them off, for Michael's tribal dance," Weir said. "You do it looking at your opponent and he walked right over to them and went through with it. It's kind of intimidating ... but it didn't work. Still, it was awesome. It's too bad Michael didn't play on Thursday because he was all fired up about it."

Campbell and Shigeki Maruyama, Thomson's captain's picks, sat out the Thursday foursomes. Unfazed by the *haka*, the Americans ploughed ahead immediately, shocking the competition by winning all five matches.

"Retief was the only guy I wasn't very familiar with," Weir said of the opening-day loss. "But it wasn't anything to do with us. We just got outplayed. We didn't make a single bogey and we lost on the 16th hole. We lost three matches one-down that first day and if we could have just got a little something more in the first matches, we might have had a better feeling."

After the disastrous first-day results, the Internationals gathered at the side of the range late in the day for a team meeting. There, Weir found out that Thomson intended to sit him and Goosen down for Friday morning's four-ball, only to run into some stiff opposition to that plan. Singh, for one, spoke up that Weir should continue to play based on his strong recent performances, that the team should rethink sitting Weir down because strong play was going to be required for any Friday rebound.

"I knew that sitting out could be an option during the week and I was OK with that," Weir said. "I knew it was part of the deal that I might have to sit out a round at some point. We were just talking as a team out there on the range. What was said made me feel very good. I knew I was playing very well and I sure did want to play. I was prepared to do what was best for the team and it sure made me feel good that the guys wanted me in there."

On the bus ride back to the team's hotel, Els stood up and offered some inspirational and encouraging words, that it was each player's duty to step up his game and not let the Cup get out of hand on the second day. "It was impressive what Ernie said," Weir commented. "He made a point of saying that we were all in this together and there was no pointing fingers and that we all needed to reach deep down and come up with the golf we knew we could play. It sure seemed to work the next morning."

Weir and Elkington clipped Lehman and Roberts 3 and 2 as the Internationals dusted themselves off to win four of the five best-ball matches. Elkington was another teammate who drew Weir's admiration, as much for his golf as his abilities to tell a joke.

"He's in a class by himself," Weir said of Elkington. "He's got those facial expressions and it's just the way he delivers a joke. I could tell the same one and people would look at me like, 'Huh?' He tells it, and everybody's falling over. It sure made for a lot of laughs on our bus trips and at dinner. And he told a couple to keep us loose while we were playing."

The Weir-Elkington victory helped the Friday-morning rally and the game was on, but only temporarily. The afternoon foursomes, where the partners combine to play just one ball, stung the visitors again. Their morning surge was completely deflated as the Americans won four of a possible five points after lunch.

Weir was partnered with Nick Price against Americans Phil Mickelson and David Duval in the afternoon.

"I thought getting paired with Nicky Price was just great for me," Weir said. "Looking all the way back to 1994 when I hit balls beside him on that range, I was thinking what an eye-opener that was for me to start some changes with my swing, and knowing that I'd never beat that guy or players of his caliber unless I made some serious changes.

"In that way, I was really excited about the pairing and I thought we'd be a great team, even before the outcome was determined."

Weir's admiration for Price's ball-striking continued that Friday. The partners were on their game from the first tee, narrowly missing birdies on the first two holes and then making them at the third and fourth to put the heat on Mickelson and Duval early.

Their teamwork then helped keep the momentum going on the par-5 fifth hole, when Price's drive took a terrible hop to the right and went down into the bushy, weeded hazard.

"It was in a terrible lie and I only moved it about 10 yards," Weir said. "The thing barely moved and Nick felt bad that he drove me into that position. He puts it back out on the fairway to 170 yards and as we were walking up, he said, 'Mike, just put it up on the green on the right level and I'll make that putt.'"

Weir did as asked, hitting a seven-iron about 18 feet from the hole, but in the meantime, Duval had put the American side in birdie range a few feet closer.

"Nick rolled it right in the middle for a beauty five and when they missed their putt, I felt it was a big dagger right there," Weir said. "We could just feel it was going our way."

The solid shot-making and putting continued right to the 14th hole, where Mickelson and Duval conceded the match and it ended 5 and 4 for the International pair, giving them the only International victory of the afternoon. Price had clearly enjoyed the experience, though he may not have been aware of its significance to his Canadian partner.

"He was rock solid," Price said after the round. "It was absolutely great to play with him today. He's been bugging me for two years for a practice round."

The partnership, in fact, was the first time Weir had ever played with Price and he said in no uncertain terms it was a thrill.

"Right after the match, we were being interviewed and I didn't want to blow any smoke to Nick because he's always a guy I've looked up to. He plays the game how I think it should be played and with class, so it was so exciting to be paired with him.

"To play as well as I did in front of him made me feel good as well. It was just an unbelievable afternoon and so much fun, to see how good a player he really is."

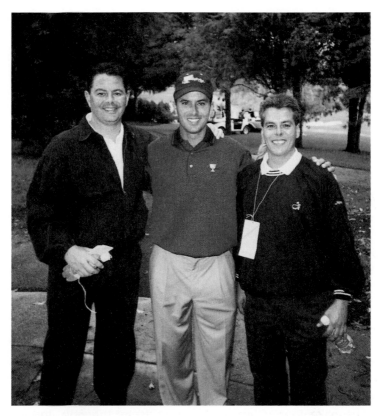

2000 Presidents Cup: Mike, with brothers Jim and Craig, after a day on the course.

"[The Americans] were a great team, and they out-putted us and out-played us," Weir said. "The key was on the greens and it seemed to be the difference all week." Despite an inspiring victory with Price as his partner, the 10-5 scoreboard count in favor of the Americans led to a rather somber Friday night. Though there were five points up for grabs on Saturday in the best-ball matches, the Internationals were five behind and the only real hope for Sunday was to grab at least three and a half, more likely four points on Saturday, in order to make it close heading into Sunday's singles matches. "At least four for a big rally," Weir said of the Saturday assignment. "And then Steve and I ran into Phil and Tom Lehman and they played unbelievable. Tom was just great. They put us down early and had us down four at one point."

Elkington and Weir made their best attempt at a comeback on the 11th. With the team honor, Weir went first from six feet and rolled in his birdie, but Lehman followed it by running his 10-footer straight in to keep the International side down four. At the 12th, Elkington made a bomb from about 60-feet for an eagle three, but Lehman again topped it by rolling home his own eagle from about 10 feet. "Any time we had a glimmer of hope in that match, Tom or Phil would end it quickly," Weir said.

The 13th hole finally went to Weir and Elkington, but the 14th was also halved, again in dramatic fashion and mostly thanks to a bunker shot by Weir that golf fans are still talking about.

With Mickelson already 15 feet from the hole for an eagle attempt, Weir stood in the bunker about 30 yards short and right of the hole on the par 5. With a severe slope moving away to his left on the green, his only option was to land the ball on the hill to the right of the green, in the rough no less, and hope it would trickle out of the long grass to the fringe, then bleed its way down to the hole. Too much bounce on the shot and the ball was racing past the pin and into the water.

"It was the only way to keep it on the green, to hope it would barely roll out of the rough, but we had to take the risk," Weir said. "As soon as I hit it, I ran up there because I couldn't see from the bunker. It came out of the rough perfectly and at one point, I thought it was going in."

The ball stopped six inches away from the hole for an easy International birdie and when Mickelson's eagle attempt failed, the halved hole was a great escape. "While we were waiting there, [U.S. team captain] Ken Venturi came over to me and whispered in my ear that the bunker shot was the greatest shot he had ever seen," Weir beamed.

It didn't, however, win the hole, and down two playing the 17th, the Internationals were up against even longer odds. From a fairway bunker 130 yards out, Mickelson's spectacular approach shot to the par 4 stopped three feet from the hole, virtually assuring the Americans of a birdie. Weir, from 120 yards in the middle of the fairway, had really only one option, to hole the next shot with his pitching wedge or call it a day.

The swing was smooth and the contact true — as it had been without fail all week — and the ball dropped to the green, leaving its pitch mark just three inches from the hole. It came to rest about four feet from the hole. His stomach fluttered a little with the shot still in the air, but Weir knew his near-miss was likely his last swing of the day. "I had it dialed in and it was flying like it was going to go right in," Weir said. "But Phil made his putt to close us out."

Weir admitted that there are few instances in the game when you stand out in the fairway knowing that your only hope is to make a golf ball go into a four-and-one-quarter-inch hole with one swing. "Things can be different in match play, though," he said. "It's amazing how acute your focus can get. But those were the kinds of shots I felt I was pulling off that week and I think it just tells me how focused I was and how important I felt it was to make shots like that. That sure was one exciting match but they deserved to beat us that day, even though we gave them a good run."

It was also typical of the continuing woe for Weir's teammates. It was another claim of four out of five points, putting the home team ahead 14-6, virtually ensuring that they would reclaim the Cup lost in 1998.

"Really, we were only left with something incredible for Sunday," Weir admitted. "Most of our guys were pretty down. There was some optimism; we thought we'd have a chance if we played great, but it didn't turn out that way. Not a lot was said, really, because we were so far behind. Everybody just knew deep down that, to make a game of it, each guy had to take care of his own business.

"If we could somehow have gained some momentum, like winning the first four out of the blocks, maybe something could have happened like you saw in the Ryder Cup, but it just wasn't to be for us."

Weir, in the fourth match of the day against fellow lefty Mickelson, was not dragged down by the dire situation. He continued to strike his irons and roll the putts squarely and it was over early, 4 and 3 for the Canadian star. "To beat a player of Phil's caliber, you need great golf and I played great golf to beat him," Weir said. "Personally, I think I just carried some momentum from the previous three weeks — but that was the best I've ever hit the ball. I don't even remember an iron shot that I hit off-line that week."

Sunday, however, the Americans just kept piling on the victories as they had all week, winning seven of the singles matches to the Internationals' four, while one match was halved. The final tally of 21 1/2 to 10 1/2 was as lopsided as it was shocking. Yet, Weir posted the best record of any International player in the event, winning three points out of a possible five in his team's miserable showing.

"I still think we should have been better but we didn't make it a close match," Weir said. "The key putts didn't fall for us and I heard from more than one guy that those greens turned out to be very deceptive. I sure felt they were tough to read. Some of the American guys I talked to said the same thing. They were very speedy, so pace was everything."

Win or lose, however, Weir said the experience was one to treasure. "The thing I enjoyed about The Presidents Cup was that it was a hard-fought competition, where everybody wanted to play well," he said. "It's a very tough competition but it was played the way the game was meant to be played, with no gamesmanship, no booing of the players, none of that stuff. Guys battled as hard as they could and we shook hands and had a beer at the end of the day. It's something I'll remember for a long time."

Even at the conclusion of the week, with the Americans celebrating their handy victory, the International team ventured over to the winners' cabin to raise a congratulatory glass. It was an episode sadly missing from the 1999 Ryder Cup. "Why would we not congratulate them?" Weir said. "Everybody knows one another very well because most of the guys playing that week are playing on the U.S. Tour."

As Mickelson had said, most members of the PGA Tour knew about Weir and his game but on the stage at The Presidents Cup, he showed it off in spades to the world with consistently great ball-striking and his deadly accurate putter.

"There's no doubt who was the best player for the Internationals this week," said NBC golf analyst Johnny Miller. "Maybe they just needed a few more Canadians. If there was a medal-play championship going on this weekend, I think [Weir] is your leader. He's playing the best golf of the week. He's a star on the rise. I think he's close to a superstar on the rise. He's very powerful, he's got a Nick Price-type of tempo to his swing. He's a great ball-striker, and an excellent putter. He has a good attitude, he's a smart guy and he's played like crazy this week."

Weir's International teammate Greg Norman was also impressed.

"He's probably one of the most underrated players I've ever played with," Norman said. "Michael has talent coming out of his ears and he's just an easygoing, likeable guy. He's got a great game of golf, and he can put the ball in a thimble with the putter. The kid's really got it. I have no doubt he's going to go a long way in the game of golf."

"Mike might not be a household name around the world but, believe me, everybody knows about him on our Tour," Mickelson said. "He's not afraid of anybody out here, nor should he be."

There seemed little danger that the reaction to and the reviews of his excellent play would affect Weir's overall outlook. Rather, he found all the raving made him feel somewhat uncomfortable.

"It's nice that guys respect your game and they'd say some of those things," Weir said. "Players who say those things have been through the process I'm going through. They know what hard work it is to get to a certain level. They've put in the time, so I guess it makes you feel better when players of that caliber say those things.

"Really, I don't want to think about what other people are saying. I just hope to continue on that trend of good play, to kind of bottle that and use it to my benefit in the future."

The future, it turned out, was close at hand.

On Top of the World

STEADY PLAY in the next two tournaments, at the National Car Rental Golf Classic in Florida and at The Tour Championship in Atlanta, produced eight straight rounds between 68 and 72. With more than $1.5 million (US) in earnings for the season and a marvelous performance at The Presidents Cup, it had been a season with plenty of merit.

But it wasn't finished. The final official-money event of the season was in Spain, at the Valderrama Golf Club near Sotogrande. The World Golf Championships' American Express Championship was a big one, worth a total of $5 million (US), with $1 million (US) for the winner. It began innocently and efficiently enough for Weir, with a 4 under par finish in Thursday's first round. He played some scratchy golf, he said, but he got the ball in the hole as he has always had a knack for doing. His ball-striking had fallen off a notch or two since The Presidents Cup and he quietly worried whether getting the maximum out of his play and only shooting 68 would be enough to contend.

During Friday's second round, the same trend emerged. Though he never wavered far from par on the day, he left the infuriating par-5 17th hole having plunked two balls into the water for a triple-bogey eight. After saving a par at the last hole, Weir signed for a round of 75 and retreated to his hotel room to take stock of the situation.

"You know, when I got back, I really couldn't find much fault in the two shots I hit in the water," Weir said. "Really, they were two of my best shots of the day but it's just that hole. I spent the whole day grinding it out, though, and I came back on the 18th with a 10-foot putt for par just to shoot 75. I felt it was a good boost, that putt, because I was 70 feet away from the hole in two and had hit my first putt 10 feet by."

With at least one good thought in his mind about the round, Weir went to his notebook to try to isolate his trouble. "I knew part of the process was that it was my sixth week in a row," Weir said. "And that counts for something. At The Tour Championship, I wasn't striking it as well and then it started getting a little worse at Valderrama."

The closed-door meeting with himself was a thorough examination of his fundamentals and when it was through, Weir arrived at one conclusion. His posture, he believed, had become sloppy. Six tournament weeks in succession had injected some fatigue into his game and he had been slouching over his golf ball just a fraction too much. That, in turn, had sent all kinds of things out of whack. To the normal eye, it would seem like such a minor thing. "But at the PGA Tour level," Weir said, "a little bit off feels like way off. Mike [Wilson] and I talk sometimes about how I can feel like a 10-handicapper when I do some things. I'm sure I can hit the ball decently in spite of things but it's not how I want it.

"In the back of my mind, I knew I couldn't be too far off. There's no way to go from The Presidents Cup kind of ball-striking to struggling that badly. I couldn't have gotten way out of whack with my mechanics. I just needed to figure it out. Usually, I do it with Mike, evaluate what we feel is going on. But he was a long way away that weekend."

The posture discovery led to an anxious night and then to a Saturday morning unlike almost any other. "Yeah, I was up that night a little bit and if there was a reason I couldn't sleep, a reason it wasn't the greatest of nights, it's because I was excited about trying out my solution in the morning," Weir said. "If there had been a night range there, I'd have gone right away, that's how badly I wanted to test it out."

At daylight, Weir was on his way to the course, a full three hours before his scheduled tee time. As meticulous as he is about details and preparation, this variance from his routine was more than just unusual. "I went to the range immediately and started seeing some results," he said. "So I drilled it in there for another 30 or 40 minutes and I had Brennan keep a close eye on my posture."

Confident the discovery would turn things around, Weir then started his regular day with breakfast in the clubhouse, some stretching and a fast trip to the physiotherapist's trailer for some assistance in getting his back and his tight neck loosened up. Then, he went back to the range and went through his regular tournament-day warm-up, confident that the scratchy golf of the first 36 holes would improve.

There aren't many days when you would feel fortunate to have the wind blowing, but on that Saturday at Valderrama, the wind was another plus for Weir's game. "I was excited about it, yeah, because if you're not striking it well, the wind's going to blow your shots off line," Weir said. "And it's so tough to recover from bad shots at Valderrama. You just have to keep it in the fairway. I figured if I was going to hit it better, I'd have a chance to shoot a good score."

He began the day eight shots away from the leader and after hitting all but one fairway and all 18 greens in the wind, Weir posted a exceptional round of 7 under 65 on a day when the average score was nearly 73. He went from eight shots back to just one behind leader Hidemichi Tanaka. "It was one of my better ball-striking rounds since The Presidents Cup," Weir said. "And then making a few putts, well, it did a great deal for my confidence going into Sunday."

Saturday, the wind was Weir's charm. Sunday, it was something more Canadian … hockey.

My strategy for Sunday was to try to duplicate Saturday. Just to keep putting the ball on the smart side of the hole and give myself the chance to shoot the best score I could. I had a great warm-up and even after putts on the first two holes spun out, I knew to just keep plugging along.

Enjoying breakfast in his hotel, Weir flipped on the television, thinking he'd kill some time before his late tee time in the final group of the day. On Skysport, they were replaying the semifinal game of the Deutschland Cup played the night before, with Canada facing off against Slovakia.

When Weir tuned in, the third period was about to begin and Canada was trailing 3-0. The game became more riveting to him as Canada chipped away at the deficit and eventually tied the game. Then, a goal with about two minutes to play put Canada ahead, leading to a tense final minute. Slovakia tied the game on a power play with one second left in regulation time.

CP PHOTO ARCHIVES (Denis Doyle)

Spain World Championship: Mike holds up the trophy after winning the American Express golf Championship at the Valderrama course in Sotogrande, Spain, November 12, 2000.

"There was a little adversity at the end of the game, but I just couldn't help but think we'd see what these Canadians were made of now, that this was what Canadian hockey was all about," Weir said. "In overtime, we pulled it out about three minutes in. It kind of pumped me up and just before I went to the golf course, I felt that's exactly the fighting spirit Canadians have in hockey and that's the kind of spirit I wanted to bring to the golf course. I just had a good sense after that hockey game that it was probably going to be a good day for Canadians."

Canada did go on to win that Deutschland Cup final and Canada's top golfer followed suit. Weir got straight to work at Valderrama on Sunday, making four birdies on the front nine. Early on the back nine, he had roared into a three-shot lead over the likes of Price, Lee Westwood, Mark Calcavecchia, Duffy Waldorf and Tiger Woods.

Weir's lead held up through the back nine, then one by one, his challengers came to the dreaded 17th hole and left shaking their heads, almost all having thrown away valuable shots. After a long delay while Westwood, Price, Calcavecchia and Woods ahead of him found the cursed water in front of the green, Weir played the hole conservatively, deciding to lay up to 77 yards in front of the green.

His lob-wedge approach then carried too far, though it was at least dry off the back side of the green. After a tricky, delicate pitch down to about four feet below the hole, Weir calmly rolled the par putt home, all but tasting a second PGA Tour victory. A final round of 69 (11 under for the week) was enough for a two-shot victory over Westwood, a $1 million (US) prize, and a three-year exemption on the PGA Tour. He also vaulted his earnings for the season to $2,547,829 (US) and all the way into sixth place on the final PGA Tour money list.

"I just felt it was an important day for Canadian golf," Weir said, when asked if he thought it was the most significant win by a Canuck golfer anywhere, any time.

While the million-dollar check was rather mind-boggling, he said it was not his priority. "The win was more special, because there was a great field and a great leaderboard," said Weir, who was named the PGA Tour's player of the month for November 2000 and in January 2001 was named the Canadian Press Male Athlete of the Year.

"Maybe the win, and my play at The Presidents Cup opened some eyes a little bit, but I don't want to worry too much about all that. I'd rather let my clubs and my game do the talking."

The talk is pretty easy to understand. It's about a talented left-hander from Bright's Grove, Ontario, whose dedication, hard work, persistence and ongoing transformation of his swing are getting him places he always wanted to be, places he dreamed of reaching back when that 13-year-old kid wrote Jack Nicklaus to find out if left really was all right.

CHAPTER 6

Swing Changes and Progress

Meet Mike Wilson

I FIRST MET Mike Wilson while I was doing some experimenting with my swing. I was practicing in the desert and staying with my good friend Brennan Little, who would eventually become my caddy, and I went to watch him get a lesson from Mike. Afterward, I talked to Mike about the golf swing and I told him that I had been reading about swing fundamentals and about the kinds of things I hoped to improve. I thought, "What the heck," and asked him to take a look at my swing. Mike and I hit it off right away. It seemed that our personalities were very compatible and he has become one of my better friends.

The strength of our relationship is that I like to delve into technical things about the golf swing and Mike does a good job of explaining things in simple terms and incorporating certain drills in order to help me get a feel for things. He's a very unique guy that way. In this chapter, Mike will walk you through the changes I've made to my golf swing since we first met on that practice tee in Palm Desert, and the reasons for those changes. In the next chapter, we have collaborated to show you some of the sound fundamentals that can help improve any golf swing.

Certainly, my swing has improved in the last four years and really, the fun part of the game for me is just seeing how good I can get. I don't know if anybody knows where or what that level is but the fun part is chasing it. I believe that if you just keep working away at it, you will get better. When I watch my own swing, I feel there are still a lot of things I can improve, and that gives me encouragement.

I hope you can find something to apply to your own golf game in these chapters. And remember, practice makes perfect.

The Old Swing

WHEN MIKE Wilson first met Mike Weir at the Indian Ridge Country Club in Palm Desert, California, in the spring of 1996, the transformation of Weir's golf swing began in earnest.

The conversation on the range that day between Wilson and Weir was pretty straightforward. "He talked about wanting to become a world-class player and a better ball-striker," Wilson recalled. "He felt that his ball-striking was what was holding him back."

On Course with Mike

I always had known how to score but my ball-striking skills were never highly reliable, or of [PGA] Tour quality. I just knew how to score, how to get it up and down with my short game and every once in a while I'd flash in a good score.

"But for the level he was trying to reach, that of a world-class player, these things were not going to work too well for him," Wilson continued. "I give him a lot of credit for knowing it, for trying to find the changes he needed, for going through the changes, and reworking his swing with a constant look at fundamentals. Mike Weir is a student of the game, a real historian. He has no desire to simply muddle through life being an average player. His goal is to be the best."

Wilson was also impressed that Weir was not looking for a quick fix, and that he was committed and determined to work, to persevere at changes and improvement.

"I think I have an ability to put things in perspective," Weir said. "The short-term setbacks, they're obviously disappointing and they hurt for the moment, but that's sports. It's a reality, except for very, very few guys. You've got to take the losses, especially in golf. Except for what Tiger's doing right now and maybe what Ben Hogan and Byron Nelson did in their day, not many players are use to winning that many tournaments. Most guys are used to winning once or twice a year, if they're playing well. The setbacks never bother me. I've always been a long-term goal-oriented kind of guy."

Weir was and is quite confident in his ability to bounce back from setbacks. An off-shoot of his determination while he's on the golf course is that he has always refused to let his disappointments hold him back.

As a kid, Weir learned to play aggressively — with a strong grip, a forward press, a pick-it-up motion during the back swing and a hard smash of the clubhead to the ground — all good things when trying to hit a puck in hockey. His athleticism allowed him to translate much of that motion to golf but it is not the way a golf club is meant to be handled if one has a high level of proficiency in mind.

As a teenager, an excellent amateur, a successful college player and a young professional golfer, Weir was a fierce competitor. It was that competitive drive that led him to the conclusion that his ball-striking flaws could be and must be addressed.

Swing habits, however, were ingrained in Weir at a young age and they were not to be unlearned in a matter of days or even weeks. Certainly not in an afternoon, during one lesson.

Wilson's first observations have offered him perspective throughout their ongoing work. "Right away when I first talked with him, I thought of how it's often a funny thing in golf, that if your fundamentals are less than ideal, it doesn't always mean you'll hit bad golf shots," Wilson said. "It's that old quote from Harvey Penick, that if you saw a tournament player with a bad grip and a bad swing, then beware, because that person had probably grooved his faults and knew how to score."

It didn't take Wilson long to see that his new student had been very good at his swing compensations, rolling them all into a move that allowed him to play very good golf.

"Mike had certainly worked out a way to compensate for his posture, grip and alignment," Wilson said. "It's what he learned as a kid. I'm certainly not saying he had a bad swing or that he was a bad player. It was not something I thought at all then because he had already won some big events."

On Course with Mike

When I started learning more about the golf swing, all the causes and effects of the swing and its motion, that's when I began to realize the faults of my own game. All those compensations really inhibited my ability to strike it on a consistent basis and that was not what I wanted for the long-term. I wanted consistency in ball-striking. The more I learned about these things, I just couldn't see why I had to settle for a game that was on one day and off the next.

To a trained eye, the left-hander's flaws and weaknesses were as prominent as the results. This created a tug-of-war that amused Wilson as much as it intrigued him.

"You looked at his swing then, which was not that great from an ideal perspective, but he had come so far," Wilson said. "That's the way he struck me. He knew he could chip, putt and hit bunker shots and fantastic pitches, but that the rest of his game didn't compare. He told me so."

And so the process began of correcting the flaws and improving the weaknesses, discovering them, learning to recognize the causes and the effects they created. Part of the process on Wilson's side of the equation since 1998 has been novel indeed. The teaching professional decided he would learn to play golf left-handed.

"I still play my rounds or the odd tournament right-handed," Wilson said. "But since then, I have only practiced left-handed. Most of it was that I wanted to learn to relate to left-handed players better, in order to communicate with them better. For me, I just felt it was a really good thing to do. Mike's short game was always so good and mine was always so bad, I figured at least he could help me get some insight into what makes his game so good."

Like his PGA Tour pupil, Wilson experienced some transitional pains as he learned a new skill. He has no intention of giving up now because it has made him a more versatile teacher.

"I just kept going with it and I'm getting more and more left-handed students," he said.

There is even some help from Weir at some of their teaching sessions.

"Every now and then he wants to look at me," Wilson said. "He has a few tips, but I don't think I'll ever be Mike Weir caliber."

In the summer of 2000, Wilson reported that his best nine-hole score as a left-handed golfer was 42. "I'm about at the level of a 10-handicapper with the short game and about a 20-handicapper with the long game," he said. "The grip, that's the hardest thing. But I hope it's not too long before I can break 80."

So when Wilson talks about fixes and corrections and trying new things, he knows first-hand they're not going to be easy. He also believes strongly that these things must be presented in pairs, something he adhered to as his work with Weir progressed.

"If you simply fix or alter the grip, you can't just leave the student with an open or closed clubface and ask him or her to get any positive feeling for change," Wilson said. "You also have to then teach the player how to adjust to the new grip by changing the swing so as to eliminate the need for compensations. This is the tricky part and the part that requires the most practice in order for it to become muscle memory."

What helped instantly was something Wilson liked very much — the athleticism of Weir's swing.

"I guess one of the ways I analyzed it was that there's always a choice," Wilson said. "You're either going to talk about geometry, all the angles of the golf swing, or you're going to talk about the physics of the swing, how to create the energy and speed. It's clear Mike always used his body well and had figured out the physics of impact from his days playing hockey. He knew how to create speed in a hockey stick or a golf club, so to me, the issue was clearly the geometry."

That's a subject that has sent many a student, young and old, running for cover. Figuring out all the planes and angles and their relationships can easily lead to headaches. And Weir and Wilson had their share while they tried to improve Weir's ball-striking.

"I remember one day Mike told me after a round that he had paid too much attention to his technique and not enough to the game and scoring," Wilson said. "We instructors call it playing golf swing, instead of playing golf. And we all know that thinking about your swing all day on the golf course isn't likely to allow you to execute many good golf shots."

Weir continually paid attention to the need for good fundamentals in the golf swing throughout the transformation. Understanding those fundamentals leads to an understanding of why it takes so long to eliminate some of those old habits, particularly in the set-up.

On Course with Mike

I guess you could call me a late bloomer. I never paid much attention to the study of the golf swing before I was 26 and that's quite a bit older than many players on the PGA Tour.

As a kid and a younger player, Weir hadn't worked extensively on swing fundamentals. It was easier to play more by feel. He found it simple to hit a golf ball without a lot of painful thinking about it. He certainly worked on his short game as a youngster and any of his friends from his Huron Oaks days will attest to it. It's something at which Weir excelled and something he practiced the most, not an unusual pattern of behavior for young players.

At the start of the process, Wilson found he was in something of an awkward position. Weir had asked for help but didn't know a lot about rotation, clubface positioning, the swing plane or what the proper sequence was. He also didn't intend to give up tour golf and return to competition two or three years down the road, and this pressure to change while continuing to play had its up times and down times.

This often resulted in many disappointing weeks and tournaments when the timing of this correction or that modification may not have been ideal. The decision to make these changes was done during a time when Weir continued to play tournament golf to support his family. Frequently, he met with tricky or uncertain situations on the golf course during a tournament round while still in the process of self-study and learning. The focus, in many of those cases, was still on Wilson's counsel or a new technique and not simply on hitting a good golf shot.

One of the technical keys that saw him through, however, was the concept of arm and forearm rotation. The bearing of arm rotation on the club head and club face position throughout the swing were crucial and with that, Weir learned what a square face is and how to recognize it just about anywhere in his golf swing. Being able to sense this position was a key in taking steps forward to improve his overall ball-striking, which is what he had asked Wilson to help him with in the beginning.

On Course with Mike

It's still difficult now, during times I really work on my swing, because you're always experimenting with things in order to try to make them better. But just like then, I still have to play through those frustrating times. I remember very well how foreign those new things felt, the feeling that the contact is not solid and how shaky the belief and trust in the process can be. I've never been tempted to just go back to my old ways. That's quite a bit different, though, than saying those old tendencies just disappear. When you get use to playing a certain way from the time you were 10 until you were 25, there have been many repetitions of those old things. I always try to keep an eye out for those habits because they creep back in once in a while. I know I'll always have to be vigilant about them.

Incorporating the ability to "feel" a square clubface into his overall proficiency for a feel-oriented game represented significant progress. Wilson recalled an example about a year into the process. "During the 1997 B.C. Open in New York, Mike had flown me in to assist him with his game," Wilson said. "We tried a few different things on the practice tee but nothing seemed to work right. Finally, with only a few minutes left before the first round he decided to just play and focus on his routine instead of his swing. He shot 67 and was in contention all week. Sometimes the only thing that will work is just focusing on your target and letting whatever happens happen."

As well as Weir's attention to fundamentals, some assistance from Utah State University sports psychologist Rich Gordin saw the left-hander through his transition days. Gordin helped him learn to think a bit differently about his game and his goals. Gordin did not meet Weir until the process of swing change and improvement with Wilson was almost a year old, but bringing the sports psychologist into the loop enhanced the entire process and streamlined communication.

Weir had always been a feel-oriented player and became a feel-oriented learner, as well. The marriage of the two is no more evident than in his now-famous pre-shot waggle, a routine he introduced at the 1998 PGA Tour qualifying school, which he won.

"Rich Gordin has said this time and again, that Mike is a real feel learner," Wilson said. "Learning by feel goes a lot further with him than any other type of learning. Now Mike knows how his club should start. By the time that Q-school began, he had tried many things and he felt he could play with this particular waggle. He liked the feel of it and after a year and a half of work on his swing, needless to say, he put on a clinic."

"When I first meet with a player, I try to tap into his learning style," Gordin said. "Mike knew that he needed to get better because he wasn't where he wanted to be with the mechanics in his swing. This was when and why he contacted Mike Wilson and upped the ante a bit, making a long-term plan with swing adjustments.

"From the psychological standpoint, the interesting part when I look at it, was determining Mike's learning style. What are the challenges, commitments, changes and frustrations involved? When you make a physical change in any sport, but especially in golf, sometimes it's 10 steps backward before it's two steps forward. That's true for an amateur and usually for a professional."

On Course with Mike

I had committed to working on many things with Mike, but my progress was anything but a smooth line. In 1995, I remember having a good year on the Canadian Tour and feeling like I was making some progress. But in 1996, I really felt like I was stumbling around until finally something good happened later in the year in Vancouver. It certainly showed me again that I was on the right track. 1997 turned into a good year on the Canadian Tour but at the qualifying school that fall, I still felt like I was working on some things that weren't panning out just yet.

And so Gordin sought to understand Weir's learning preferences and tendencies and once he had assembled enough information, began to consult with Wilson on methods.

"Mike, like many players on the PGA Tour, has many ways to put information into his system: visual, kinesthetic [feel], and by repetitions," Gordin said. "Of course, there's the cognitive, too, which is talking and explaining. Of those, Mike prefers, like many great players, to get the picture and get the feel and then do a lot of repetitions.

"You don't learn to swing a club by talking about it. You don't say, 'That thought good,' you say, 'That felt good.' That's how Mike is. Players are smart and they want input. Once they get the feel, it really clicks. That's what we mean by those 'a-ha' moments."

The process, which had already begun, was not simply a list of "a-ha" moments. There were many annoying days during which things did not seem smooth at all. Crooked shots, confusing feel and stubborn old habits were frequent visitors to practice sessions and competitive rounds. Gordin said this was expected.

"Mike made a commitment to do this with Mike Wilson," Gordin said. "With that comes some setbacks and frustrations. The thing about Mike Weir, though, is that once he commits to change, he commits. It's not 99 per cent, it's 100 per cent. He's got a pretty good tolerance for change. Some people, when they don't see results, they become easily frustrated.

"But Mike Weir and Mike Wilson, they had a long-term plan they agreed to work on and dealing with the frustration was built in. They knew there would be some but when you see some results, it makes it easier to take."

What Gordin means by results is the little victories, a practice session or even a tournament or practice round with a few good swings, or a day with better ball flight or nine holes where the ball contact felt much more solid. It's any number of little signs that tell you that you're on the right path, that you're getting closer to what you're trying to accomplish.

"Oh yes, it's those little victories that are important," Gordin said. "The big [tournament] victories come from a lot of good swings, and also from a lot of hard work and good mental training. In a tournament, you won't hit or putt it perfectly all day. You have to keep an even keel through the mis-hits.

"I've always liked that quote from Bobby Jones, that 'he who plays his mis-hits best, wins.' Golf is like no other sport that way. Mike approached these things as a challenge, not a hurdle. That's how he keeps things on course. He's not prone to be anxious when he learns. He has patience. Much of it is the trust between him and Mike Wilson. There are two things necessary in that kind of relationship. The first is trust and the second is that Mike Weir feels that Mike Wilson can help him. They have those things and now they have a chance to do something pretty special."

On Course with Mike

I've always thought our relationship had a chance to be something special with Mike [Wilson]. He's helped me more on how to swing the club correctly while maintaining my skill at getting the ball in the hole. We have these moments on the range all the time, where we'll be experimenting with something. I'll find something and he'll say, "That's exactly what I hoped you'd come across," or "That's exactly what I was thinking." We find we're saying that a lot.

"There's one moment that always comes to mind instantly, from the 1999 BellSouth Classic in Atlanta," said Wilson. "Mike was starting to play pretty well but he needed a tip, a spark, to get him going. He said he was struggling with his swing just a bit, because it was feeling a little long and a little loose. I just asked him to be sure not to let his right arm get above his left shoulder during his backswing, so as to eliminate any lifting of his arms. He had already been focusing on the correct lower-body motions, so this tip helped him to tie it all together quickly. He said right away his swing felt shorter and more together and his power-level really jumped. He finished in a tie for fifth that week and it turned out to be a great confidence booster."

As Gordin joined Weir's support group and brought himself up to speed in the process, he discovered quickly that Weir and Wilson had a certain synchronization that had become finely tuned.

"I'm convinced they got on the same page pretty quickly," Gordin said. "It's so important between an instructor and student. It's true at the amateur level as well, though the amateur will often take one thing and work on it until the next time they meet, and by then he's made it into 10 [problems].

"The professional, however, will take 10 things and boil them down to one thing. The greatest athletes in the world make the complex simple."

What was not simple about the changes and improvements Weir and Wilson were trying to incorporate was Weir having to switch from learning mode to playing mode, since he had not given up competing in tournaments. But the switch was neither automatic nor easy.

"I was fortunate to be in Palm Springs at the 2000 Bob Hope Chrysler Classic," Gordin said. "There, I observed Mike and Mike at work. I was just there watching, seeing them in action. When you're doing intense work on drills and swing technique, it's a distinct training mode. All that work on technique was happening, and then Mike Weir had to turn that off and go play in the Bob Hope. We talked about that. It's like a light switch. It has to be like a light switch. The key is to turn it off when you're trying to play. You can't be working on technique when you're trying to get the ball into the hole. It's so very difficult for any player to switch. It's really the only time I've ever seen Mike Weir's frustration level go up a hair."

On Course with Mike

I wasn't always successful at doing that (switching from learning to playing), but it was a necessary element of what I was trying to do. My practice in the past was not thinking much because I just knew how to get it in the hole. Often, just going back to that benefited me in those times: when you're on the golf course, just worry about scoring. It took a while for us to figure out — and it's become very important now — that when Mike comes to tournaments, we focus more on maintenance than change. Big changes at tournaments don't work for me. I'd rather do more of that kind of work in the off weeks or in the off-season, when I can visit Mike and spend an entire week and really get into it.

Frustrated or not, Weir has maintained enough perspective to know how important the people in his support group — especially Wilson and Gordin — are.

"I'm so fortunate to have Mike and Rich helping me," Weir said. "They're not guys who are there and gone and you never talk to them until the next time you see them. They've become good buddies and they're so enthused when I'm working with them. They're excited about things that have happened in my career. They've been through this journey with me and they've become really good friends, too. They're really involved with the whole deal."

The "whole deal," of course, means the before and the after.

If you were to compare Weir's old set-up and swing to any number of classic set-ups and swings, he would not have measured up very well in 1996. Certainly, he had some ability to hit the ball a great distance and to keep it under control, but it's unlikely that Weir was a better ball-striker than his college or amateur opponents from the past. His short game, a very special talent indeed, saw him through many a round or match, as did his determination.

The results on his résumé — several important amateur titles and accomplishments, a Canadian Tour victory and many close calls as a professional — did not cloud Weir's perspective, leading him to the 1996 meeting with Wilson. The dramatic shift in the path of his career began as a straightforward thought to abandon much of the old and unreliable and adopt something new and consistent.

The Old Set-up

Posture

Weir's hips would always sit too level to the ground, as a rule, and his belt buckle was not lower than his tail bone at address. Level hips led to a back that was too rounded. The more rounded your back is at address, the less you're able to make a good shoulder turn. Level hips often lead to soft legs and that leads to instability during the backswing. This did not afford Weir much stability in his lower body as he prepared to begin his golf swing.

Grip

Weir gripped the golf club in the palm of his right (higher) hand instead of down more in his fingers. Compounding this flaw in the top hand was that his bottom (left) hand was too strong, too far underneath the grip on the club. This did not allow him to properly hinge his wrists during the motion of the swing. One of the keys to a good swing is hinged wrists and rotating forearms, and Weir's old grip allowed him to do neither very well. His old grip also forced the start of his swing to be more "around the corner," another of the many compensations that had been ingrained in his set-up and swing.

Alignment

Weir set up to his golf ball with shoulders open. This starting position complicated things even further, as a shoulder turn was even more difficult to make because he had farther to turn than he would from a square position. The first part of his backswing would just get him to square. He then had to continue to turn from there to complete his backswing.

Poor Posture:
Too much bend at the waist makes it hard to turn and also leaves the ball too far away. Weir's rounded shoulders and rounded back are moderate in this example compared to how they used to be before 1996.

The Swing Flaws

Though it may seem unduly harsh, Weir's old swing could be described as "rolly, twisty and lifty."

The roll refers to the way Weir would begin his backswing, by rolling the club to the inside. The twist refers to his leg work during the backswing, where he lacked proper stability. The lift refers to the way he would complete his backswing.

With his strong grip and the slight forward press that usually marked the beginning of the swing, the hands immediately moved away from his body and the club came inside.

On the way back, the right (top) hand would bend backwards which tended to put the clubface into a shut position. Open shoulders inhibited a full and proper turn, and by the time Weir was done with what turn he could make, the club was barely more than halfway to the top. To compensate for never being fully wound behind his golf ball, his arms tended to lift the club to the top, leaving his right arm pointing straight up at the top of the backswing and the club in a very shut position. The lifting motion to reach the top varied with each club — with the wedge there wasn't so much motion but with longer clubs like the driver, there was a lot of lift.

Weir's ball-striking performance then became a day-to-day thing — based on how he would lift the club on a particular day. Many other things caused the inconsistencies but the result of most of his long swings was that on the way down to the ball, the angle of approach of the clubhead was very steep. The result of this steep angle was a deep divot and the need for another compensation in order to get the ball up in the air.

One side effect of this steep angle of attack was some back trouble for Weir in college. With a clubface that attacks steeply and is shut, you often lean backwards to try to get the club down to the ball. This compensation, along with the twisting motion already present, puts great stress on the spine.

"Mike is a very athletic guy, who generated a lot of clubhead speed," Wilson said. "So when he had his hips turning as actively as they did underneath him and then the spine bending backwards slightly to help the ball into the air, there was a lot of sheer force on his spine."

With so many variables, Weir's swing was less reliable under the pressures of competition. Overall, his ball flight was extremely low and his ball never stayed in the air too long. Carrying three-irons over water was

always possible, but the landing on the other side wasn't always predictable, leaving these kinds of shots very uncomfortable for him. Other tendencies included an equal assortment of thin and fat shots, depending on the day's particular compensations, and also hitting hooks with the driver.

The Benefits

As has been noted, Weir's swing carried him through some important stages. Despite the number of undesirable characteristics, there were some advantages. One was that it's always better to have less hand action through the impact zone than too much, and Weir was good in that department with his knack for good timing at impact.

His old swing was also graded high for a proper release and keeping excess rotation out of the forearms. In his old form and new, Weir has shown an ability to generate excellent power in his swing, certainly a carry-over from his adeptness at other sports. Wilson believes that Weir's hockey background contributed greatly to his dynamic, athletic, and aggressive move at a golf ball and not surprisingly, driving the ball was frequently a strength during the good periods of his game.

Through the hitting zone, Weir was very efficient because of those power factors and also because he was disciplined enough to usually stay behind the ball during the swing.

Low Ball Flight and Other Effects

With a very low ball flight, Weir was left in some uncomfortable positions on the golf course. Hitting a three-wood off the ground to par 5s, or simply carrying a hazard or front bunker was a very challenging predicament.

On Course with Mike

At the 1999 Western Open when I was playing with Tiger Woods, I hit a five-wood over some trees and onto the green at a par 5. In my earlier days, there was no way I'd ever be able to pull off this shot — my ball would never have been high enough in the air.

Consistent iron play was also a task, simply because of the angle of his clubhead's attack.

And as mentioned the old swing and low ball flight always left Weir at risk for lower back trouble.

The New Swing

Set-up Positions

Weir has now returned his shoulders to a line parallel to his target, or square. With that change, the ball position has shifted slightly back in his stance.

The grip now has Weir holding the club more in the fingers of his right (top) hand as opposed to his previous grip, when it was toward the palm of his hand. The left (bottom) hand is now sitting more on top of the grip, in a weaker position than before.

"When we first started to work on positioning his left hand more on the top of the shaft, we had mixed results," Mike Wilson recalls. "It was during the 1998 Nissan L.A. Open and it worked perfectly on the practice tee. The ball had more height and more speed as well. We went out and played a practice round with Lanny Wadkins and Dan Forsman and Mike hit it great. Unfortunately, during the tournament, it proved to be a bit too new to him because he missed the cut, mainly due to too much attention being paid to the new grip."

There is also a dramatic change in posture for Weir's new set-up, featuring hips that are now tilted more forward, toward the ball, his belt buckle now lower than before and his tail bone higher. In concert with this, he has adopted a straighter spine, giving the sense of feeling taller in his chest. This "feeling tall" posture has been a key.

Now as Weir prepares to swing the club, he is much more balanced. His weight feels more like it's on his left side at address than before — though Wilson says it's simply closer to the ideal 50-50 than it's ever been — since Weir used to have more pressure on his right foot at address. He has also adopted a slightly wider stance — to enhance stability — than several years ago, something he started to use in competition in Phoenix in 1999.

In general now, with his tail bone up, a taller feeling in the chest and a straighter spine, Weir has transferred more pressure to the front of his legs and his quadriceps muscles. This has greatly enhanced the stability in his lower body and placed him in a better position to unleash the power of his swing.

Swing Keys

The ready feeling leaves Weir in a rock-solid position as he begins the take-away move. He likes to refer to this feeling as "gripping the ground," which simply means that he is well-grounded, especially with his left leg. Among all the improvements and adjustments he's made since 1996, developing quieter, more solid legs is high among the reasons for his progress.

Trying to keep the grip close to the left (back) leg at the beginning of the take-away, Weir has the club and his hands in one piece as he moves the club back exactly on the desired swing plane. The overriding thought for the take-away is to keep it all in one piece — the shoulders, arms and club — and working as one piece.

The result is a swing that's more square throughout, one that has good balance, one that doesn't have to roll or twist to compensate. Once it reaches the top, he simply tries to unwind his body from the ground up. This sequence of hips, shoulders, arms and club leaves Weir free to deliver his athletic power to the ball, with the same aggressive thinking he has always used.

Key Concepts — The Waggle

One of Weir's new key concepts is the one-piece take-away move, one that keeps his club on the proper plane. This is where his waggle (some call it half a practice swing) developed — it's a move he is now well-known for, one that has become his trademark.

"Well, it began as an attempt to keep the club from rolling too much and to keep him tall off the ball," Wilson says. "He has worked on many things like that to promote the correct feeling and this has been the result."

Weir tried many versions of the waggle and went through many days and practice sessions of trial and error to find just the right things to incorporate into it. The development of his short practice move before every full swing is a rehearsal and a reminder that the balance and the proper plane are paramount.

"Once he got used to this waggle, he really started killing it [the ball]," Wilson says. "He continues to say it's the best it's ever felt, hitting the ball. He can just feel how square he is and how much balance he has. It has really done wonders for how he hits the golf ball, and also for his confidence."

Drills

Left Foot Back Drill

Wilson believes this is one of the best drills. Weir stands very closed, with right foot forward and left foot back, as a lefty. This promotes the feeling that the club is coming more from the inside and on the correct plane. A good feeling with this drill is also to keep your shoulders slightly closed at address as well.

Side-hill Lies

Weir works frequently with side-hill lies, always with the ball above his feet. This gives the feeling of a flat, manageable plane.

Pre-set Drill

Weir will get set over his ball, then simply cock his wrists back to where they're fully set, then take the swing from there. This gets him thinking of the correct swing plane, the squareness of the clubface and also keeps him from lifting the club during his take-away.

It's a drill that Mike Wilson learned from David Leadbetter during the time he spent working at Leadbetter's academy. Wilson introduced this drill into Weir's practice routine very early in their relationship.

Start Forward Drill

Placing a ball on a tee, Weir addresses the ball with a seven-iron, lifts the club and moves it forward of the ball. He then sweeps it back over the ball

The Waggle:

From address (1), Weir takes the club back low (2), (3) and deliberately, paying strict attention to placing the club and shaft on the proper plane (4), (5). He stops this swing rehearsal about halfway back and does a visual check (4), (5) to confirm the proper feel. From this position, Weir resets the club in address behind the ball and then pulls the trigger on his full swing without much hesitation.

to about half-way back, then makes the shot. This creates the feeling of momentum in the golf swing, also giving the feeling of the face being in a more open position coming into impact.

Speed-up Drill

With an iron, Weir begins to swing the club back and forth but only about halfway back and halfway forward. He gradually accelerates this pendulum-type motion until the club is whipping quickly back and forth and he cannot go any faster. The total time of this drill might be 15 seconds. The purpose is to keep the arms connected to the body, to keep them swinging together, which is essential for a golf swing that can be repeated time after time. Picking up speed as he goes also helps him gain the necessary acceleration needed in the swing.

Speed-up Drill:
While limiting the forward and backward swing, try to keep the clubhead below the shoulders and gradually speed up until you cannot go any faster. This drill promotes keeping the arms connected to the body.

Matzie Drills

The swing aid with the molded grip, a yellow club head and the crooked shaft is used by many players. Weir has a left-handed model, which gives him his desired hand position to start. The way the Matzie's toe is weighted helps him naturally rotate his forearms.

The Matzie:
The weighted, yellow clubhead outline on the end of a crooked shaft allows the weight of this swing aid to be easily felt in the grip, which is molded for the fingers.

Impact Bag

A big swing aid bag, about 18 inches tall, stuffed full of towels helps Weir freeze his position at impact. The goal, of course, is not to bash the bag down the fairway. The bag absorbs energy and, used properly, will help a player feel where his body, legs and arms are at impact by simply stopping them there.

Impact bags and the Matzie can be used together to combine some of the correct feelings.

Fitness Aspects

CONSIDERING HIS previous bouts with back pain, and also the increased pressure and demands from his lower body and legs, stretching has become part of Weir's daily routine. He works diligently to keep his back and legs, especially the hamstrings, flexible and warmed up, body parts that can help increase his range of motion.

Weir focuses on core conditioning, working on his stomach, lower abdominal and leg muscles, as well as his lower back. He has incorporated a Swiss ball into his training as well, allowing him to include stretching drills.

These are just part of his general fitness regimen. That routine includes running between three and five miles, three times per week, and a weight-training program that concentrates on strength training, especially in the particular areas mentioned. Weir's weight-room sessions typically last anywhere from 45 to 75 minutes.

All of his fitness training is as much geared toward performance as it is toward injury prevention and it is thoroughly individualized, an aspect Weir believes is essential.

"If you're going to train in this way, you need to get a conditioning program that's right for you," he said. "Everybody is different. Other PGA Tour players are not necessarily doing the same kinds of exercises because everybody's body type is different. You've got to determine what's right for you. Don't just randomly adopt something because a certain person is doing it."

An overall fitness routine has become an intergral part of Weir's everyday life since he met and began working with Mark Verstegen in 1998.

Mark moved on to Tempe, Arizona, and opened his Phoenix-area fitness company, Athletes' Performance, which specializes in both fitness and nutrition and he has helped Weir develop a focus and a plan in these areas. A more educated approach to his training and to his overall goal of maintaining great health has been the result.

Dramatic strides in Weir's training, even his performance, is supplemented by good eating habits. If you have watched him play, it's likely you've seen him walking down a fairway munching on something.

Weir pays strict attention to his calorie intake, usually to make sure he's getting enough. The stress of competition, the rigors of tournament golf — walking the course and practice sessions on the range — require plenty of energy, so eating is important.

"For my build, I can't afford to lose much weight," he said. "And when I go to work with Mike, I really try to take in more calories because I might be out on the range for five or six hours at a time. Even for those kinds of days, I'll pack some food and plenty of water in my bag."

Attention to nutrition has been part of Weir's routine for many years. When he first started playing golf professionally, he not only paid attention to his diet, but often charted what he ate to see if there was any correlation to how he felt.

On Course with Mike

I always laugh at the old saying "at the turn, take a hot dog, make a double," but there might be something to it. A big meal between nines is not the key to performance. Being full isn't going to help. Half a sandwich would be better, and spread it out during the round. I think eating on the golf course is important, and I prefer to do it more frequently because it helps your blood-sugar level stay constant. The key is not to be hungry out there. I often pack a peanut butter and jelly sandwich in the bag with a health bar and some kind of nutritional drink or meal-replacement drink. And I like to drink plenty of water while I'm playing.

"I'm meticulous about the details, so I did some experimenting with that to see what I could find out about myself. But it's not always about being meticulous. It's about making sure that you're eating healthy food.

"Chocolate bars and sodas at the turn will help you less than drinking water or a sports drink and eating constantly throughout the round. And in terms of regular diet, a steady menu of burgers and fries simply isn't as good for you as things like chicken and vegetables."

Weir is not alone in his attention to training, fitness and nutrition, leaving no doubt that golf is clearly much more of a sport than ever. "I'm sure everyone knows about Tiger and David Duval and their commitment to working out," Weir said. "But other guys have started to devote a lot of attention to it too, like Vijay Singh, Stu Appleby and Justin Leonard. Overall, more and more guys on tour are starting to do something about fitness. It might not always be weight training, but stretching and exercise have become very important."

Teaching Aids

- The Matzie is a practice "club" with several features: a molded grip that positions the hands correctly on the club; a crooked shaft; a yellow clubhead that's more an outline of a clubhead than anything you'd use to hit a ball; and a weighted toe that is easily felt in the grip. The Matzie is popular because it allows a player to do "mindless practice." The molded grip and overall design of the club allows the golfer to grip properly and take a proper swing without having some 20 swing thoughts in his or her head.

- The impact bag is very useful because it helps to eliminate the "wristiness" or slapping at the ball so common in amateur golfers.

■ A small ball is one of Weir's most helpful teaching aids. The one he uses has the appearance of a small soccer ball and is soft enough to stay between the arms, even when it's squeezed a little. Placed there, the ball allows him to train muscles in the upper arms and shoulders to maintain a constant distance between his elbows throughout the swing. In the same way during putting practice, placing the ball between the arms helps Weir keep his stroke all in one piece, giving him the feeling of everything moving together.

■ A small convex mirror is also something Weir uses during practice. Most often it is placed directly behind his intended line of ball flight. This allows him to get feedback on his posture and alignment with a quick glance — when the eyes of his coach or caddy aren't readily available.

■ The putting center, which is in the basement in Weir's Draper, Utah home is also important. Most of his short game work, especially on the greens, is done at home. In his basement, he had fast carpet installed to give him the feeling of quick greens. There are mirrors on both walls so that he can analyze and work with his putting set-up, with a mind toward maintaining a consistent posture and alignment. And of course, there's something to be said for privacy when you're working.

CHAPTER 7

The Fundamentals

Introduction

I F ONLY learning the game of golf could somehow be different than all the other disciplined things in life. Unfortunately, or fortunately, a strict adherence to the fundamentals or basics will save you a lifetime of frustration through trial and error. Mike Wilson, Mike Weir's instructor since 1996, sees four important categories worthy of study.

Posture

Correct posture is the cornerstone of the swing. Without the right posture, you will find it almost impossible to create any consistency to your set-up. By studying and practicing your set-up, you will find that your body will naturally begin to engage the right set of muscles. If your posture is correct you will engage the muscles in the front of the legs and the lower back, and your chest will "be tall." This is a very athletic position in which a golfer can move easily.

Correct Posture:
Notice Weir's hips tilted forward, his belt buckle low and his
"tall-feeling" chest.

> ## On Course with Mike
> I like to feel solid in my legs and upright with my chest. This makes me feel ready for action and ready to make an athletic swing.

There are also two kinds of posture, static and dynamic. Static posture is your posture at address, before the swing. Dynamic posture is your posture during the swing. Most amateur golfers start with poor static posture (angles, hips and knees), making it difficult to swing the club properly or to move correctly. If you start with poor posture, you are probably not in balance and are likely to move around a great deal during the swing. Too much head movement is usually the result of poor posture at address. The old comment, "You lifted your head," is one that Mike Wilson hears all the time. But Wilson insists it's better to think about good posture than simply keeping your head still. Beginning with good static posture gives you a greater chance of having good dynamic posture.

Grip

While it has been said many times before, a correct grip is important because it is your only connection to the club. The grip is consistently misunderstood simply because most golfers do not understand the role that the hands should play in the golf swing. The hands should remain quiet throughout the swing and especially through the impact area. In order for the hands to do this, they must be positioned properly on the club, holding it more in the fingers and less in the palms. When the hands are properly positioned on the club, most amateur players feel as though they don't have any control and it's likely why so many of them try to grip it more in their palms or in the middle of their hands.

Most players would be much better off using a 10-finger or so-called baseball grip. This is simply much easier to learn and to repeat properly. One of the oldest teaching aids instructors have used in order to teach the feeling of a good grip is to have a student grip a yardstick. By gripping a yardstick, students automatically place the club into the fingers properly instead of into the palms.

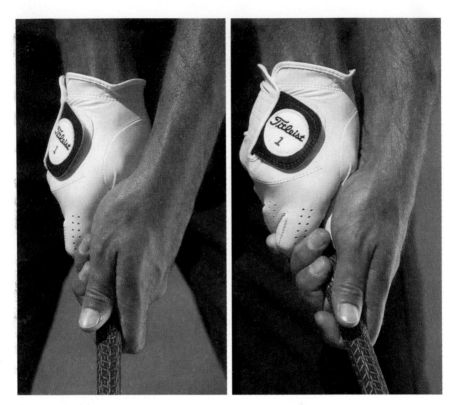

Grip:
The club is properly held in the fingers, not the palms.

> **On Course with Mike**
> I like to feel my left hand more on the top of the club than I used to. This has helped me greatly improve the strike on my irons.

Ball Position

There always seems to be a question about the proper ball position in order to hit a wedge, a driver, or any other club. For normal shots, the ball should be positioned opposite the spot between your shirt buttons and armpit.

"I was always taught to put the ball back in my stance for my short irons and the ball forward in my stance for my long irons and my woods," Wilson says. "In my opinion, that was just old advice from another era."

Ball Position:

Weir, with driver in hand, demonstrates good ball position at the spot opposite his right armpit (A). You can also see that the end of his club is pointed approximately at the middle of his body and that his hands are not ahead of the ball. For a five-iron (B), the ball position is opposite the spot between his shirt buttons and armpit. For a wedge (C), ball position is slightly back of (B) but never farther back than opposite the shirt buttons. Weir also places irons on the ground, one to help him with foot alignment and the other to help with ball position.

Ball Position:

The view from behind illustrates that ball position varies with club selection. With the driver, which Weir has in hand, the ball will always be farthest from the body. With five-iron or wedge, which rest against his right thigh, you can see the approximate ball position. Keep in mind that the shorter the iron, the closer the ball will be.

In order to accommodate the old equipment such as hickory shafts and older-style golf courses (where run-up shots were far more common), these old rules may have worked great. With today's equipment and the newer style of golf courses, a more sound approach is to have the ball opposite the spot between your shirt buttons and your armpit.

The farthest back the ball should be played for a normal swing is the middle of your stance, or opposite your shirt buttons. This would be the spot to position the ball for your wedge. The driver, on the other hand, ought to be closer to the spot opposite your armpit. Remember that longer clubs, such as fairway woods/metals and longer irons should be closer to the driver spot while shorter irons will be closer to the wedge spot.

It should not vary more than that, since the actual hitting area where the club strikes the ball is really only three or four inches wide. This also simplifies matters greatly for beginners and junior players. There are enough elements to be aware of in a good golf swing and consistent ball position simply eliminates one more variable.

Alignment

More often than not, when an instructor talks to a student on the practice tee about alignment, there are looks ranging from cringing fear to silent embarrassment. Most of those students probably believe that alignment will be measured or determined by some equation of astro-physics or survey engineering. It's really none of that. Put more simply, there's a better word for alignment — aim.

Alignment:
To help you discover if you're correctly aligned in the lower body, take an iron and hold it on your thighs (1) or hips. The end of the club (2) should be pointed at the target, leaving shoulders, thighs and feet all aimed at the same spot. Hip and thigh alignment are in concert with shoulder alignment.

Alignment:
An easy way to discover if you're correctly aligned with the shoulders is to take an iron and hold it across your chest with crossed arms (1). Then simply look down the line of the iron (2) and (3) to see if it is pointed at the target.

One of the most common problems seen in many students is that they simply fail to align properly. Their eyes are looking at the target but their club, their feet and their shoulders are usually aimed somewhere else. Poor aim can be the result of a swing flaw in which the player compensates by aiming to accommodate the flaw. Left-handed players who frequently hit big slices will probably find themselves lined up, or aimed, too far to the right. Poor aim can also be the result of poor ball position. Ideally if you've worked hard on your posture, having proper alignment is easily achieved. This is because good posture promotes a square stance where your feet, hips, and shoulders all are aimed at your target.

Good aim is nothing more than that.

Application

Driving

Set-up Differences

There's not a student anywhere who would not want to hit their driver better. A great drive will set up the hole perfectly and is also very gratifying. Here are a couple of tips to improve your set-up position when hitting your driver. First of all, make sure that at least 60 per cent of your weight is on your back foot at address. Second make sure that the end of your club's grip points at the middle of your body.

The reason you'd like to have the grip pointing that way is that it helps promote the sweeping action necessary for a driver swing, allowing you to hit up on the ball. If the end of the grip is not pointing at the middle of your body, you may be prone to press forward with your hands. That causes more of a chopping action with the driver — you've seen the divots on par 5 tee boxes — as opposed to the preferable sweeping action.

On Course with Mike

When I swing with the driver, I really stay behind the ball. It allows me to achieve incredible power — it's one of my best assets.

Driver Set-up:
With the driver, Weir is set up with about 60 per cent of his weight on his left foot (1). In both photos, notice ball position opposite his right armpit and that the end of his club is pointed at the middle of his body. Hands (2) remain behind the ball, making it easier to sweep the club away and to stay behind the ball through the downswing.

Swing Keys

There are two swing keys that will help you to hit your driver long and true. First of all, make a full turn on your back swing, turning your back to the target and coiling into your back leg. This will help you to achieve maximum torque, helping to store the power you're about to unleash on the ball. Second, make sure that on the downswing, your head is behind the ball. This is especially important at impact. You simply will not find a good driver who has their head ahead of the ball at impact.

Poor Driver Set-up:
Hands ahead of the ball (1), or forward pressed, lead to more of a chopping action with the driver and make it harder to sweep the club back and through the ball. In this poor set-up position, notice also how the weight has shifted to the right foot (2) and how that will make it difficult to remain behind the ball through impact.

Fairway Woods

Fairway woods have never been more popular. In this day and age, you find many professional golfers discarding their one- and two-irons and replacing them with fairway woods. This is because there is a great variety of clubs that have many desirable characteristics available to professional players today.

Fairway Woods:
More and more players, Weir included, are including in their bags
fairway woods of various lofts and removing long irons.

Finding the Right Combination

The most important thing to remember when choosing your fairway woods is that the proper combination of loft and shaft flex will give you the best performance. If you are a low-ball hitter, then you want to choose either a seven- or nine-wood in order to help you get the ball up into the air. If you are a very high-ball hitter then perhaps a four- or five-wood would better suit your game.

Remove Those Long Irons

Many professionals also prefer fairway woods to long irons because of the forgiveness they offer. A mis-hit one- or two-iron might only travel 85 per cent of the distance required to pull off a shot while a mis-hit seven-wood might travel 95 per cent of the correct distance. Most players prefer the 95 per cent!

Long Irons

Keep It Smooth

If you happen to be a low-handicap player, you might prefer to use your long irons, depending on the courses you play. One of the common flaws associated with long-iron play is that most players try to force the swing instead of just letting it happen. So here's some good advice: Keep it smooth with those long irons, especially in your take-away. A quick or jerky take-away will often ruin the best of efforts when trying to play a shot with a long iron.

If you can mimic the same kind of action used to strike a fairway wood or your driver, you will be far closer to the correct swing for a long iron. In keeping with that, don't try to play long irons with a ball position in the middle of your stance. This one belongs opposite the spot between your shirt buttons and your armpit, forward of the center of your stance, so that you can benefit from the sweeping action of the swing and get cleaner contact.

Middle Irons

The middle irons, such as five-, six- and seven-irons, are great clubs to practice with when learning a new technique. This is because they promote good fundamentals and especially good posture. If you are going to the practice tee to work on your swing, it's wise to do the bulk of your work with your mid-irons.

"When we are working on swing technique on the practice tee, Mike and I do a lot of work with the mid-irons," Mike Wilson said. "Once he begins to swing them well and hit good shots, we move on to long irons and then to woods. I strongly advise amateur players to do the same."

Long Irons:
A low take-away is accomplished by a sweeping move backward and by resisting the temptation to pick the club up with the hands. By turning the shoulders and keeping arms extended, the clubhead remains close to the ground.

Long Irons:
Weir's ball position for a long iron is slightly behind the driver position. This will allow him to take advantage of the swing's sweeping action, making it easier to get a long iron shot airborne.

Par-3 Magic

You'll also find that by practicing your middle irons, you will become a very good par 3 player. The average par 3 today measures between 125 and 175 yards. This 50-yard variance falls right into the range most golfers hit their mid-irons, so it's only natural that the more you practice with them, the more confidence and success you're bound to have.

Over the past couple of seasons, Mike Weir has not been a consistent par 3 player on the PGA Tour, but at the 2000 Memorial Tournament, where he finished fourth, he was 3 under par for the week on par 3s. That is a great improvement and another glimpse of his progress.

Approach Irons

The Scoring Clubs

The approach irons, anything between the eight-iron through the sand wedge, are known as the scoring clubs. On a particular day when you're hot with these clubs, you're bound to shoot a low number.

Knock 'em Stiff

An important tip to remember when hitting your pitching wedge or sand wedge is to zero in on your target. So many players simply hit *toward* the green instead of finding an exact target. When this is brought to the attention of many students on the practice tee, their response is often: "I will be lucky to hit the green, let alone get near the pin."

Often times, the analogy of an archer, who's taking aim at a target with a bow and arrow, gets the point across. Won't the archer aim at the bull's eye and not just at the target? Even though he knows he probably won't hit the bull's eye, he will still aim at it. The same is true for golf.

Don't Force the Distances

One of Mike Weir's true strengths is using his approach clubs with deadly accuracy. This is because he refuses to try to force in an eight-iron when a seven-iron should be the club. If you try to force the distances in your short irons, you will most likely over-swing and mis-hit the shot.

Three-quarter Swing:
Weir won't force his distances and instead, makes a controlled yet aggressive three-quarter swing. His backswing is not even close to parallel with the ground (1), yet the speed of the downswing is purposeful (3) and the finish is just short of full (8).

Approach Iron — Full Swing:
Weir's backswing is just short of
parallel to the ground (1). He
fully uncoils through the ball (3)
and has a full finish (7). Instead
of trying to overpower the ball
with short irons in an in-between
yardage situation, Weir often
takes the next club up with this
kind of swing.

It's All About Distance Control

The next time you play, try using one more club than you normally do and then just make a nice, normal swing. Keep your tempo the same, maintain a regular backswing length and swing in control. You're bound to find the results very rewarding.

Keep It Short and Compact

You'll also find that Mike Weir makes a short and compact swing when hitting his short irons. This also creates a repeatable motion that is highly reliable under pressure.

The Short Game

Pitching

One of the hardest shots to learn in golf, and also to teach, is the garden-variety pitch shot. The main reason is that it requires less than a full swing. When less than a full swing is required, whatever compensations have been present in full swings become less predictable, leading to a wide variety of results.

Getting the technique right is the road to good pitching. When it comes to hitting a pitch shot or a short, lofted shot that flies more than it rolls, there are a few things to keep in mind. First, try to picture the shot you want to hit and pick out a spot on the green where you want the ball to land. You may want to use a practice session just for this, to determine what kind of short swing with your pitching club (usually a wedge or a sand wedge) will carry the ball five yards, 10 yards and so on.

When trying to implement such a shot, after picking out your approximate landing spot, try to imagine tossing a ball onto the green underhanded. This underhanded motion is perfect for simulating a pitching swing. Once you have visualized the shot, simply use a narrow stance and play the ball forward in your swing. The technique is similar to a chip shot, only with a little more turn and a little wrist hinge.

Feel the wrist slightly hinge on the back swing and then turn your chest through to the target. If you've seen Mike Weir on television or at a tournament, you know he is a great pitcher of the ball. His left foot stays grounded and he turns beautifully through each shot.

Poor Pitching Technique:
If you find your wrists flipped over during pitch shots, as Weir
demonstrates, you'll find your results very unpredictable. Players who
exhibit this broken-down form are usually trying to scoop the ball off
the ground or have suddenly tried to accelerate or decelerate their club.

Pitching Set-up:
Using a narrow, slightly open, stance, Weir demonstrates good set-up.
From this position, quiet hands and turning your chest through to the
target usually brings good results.

Chipping

Good chippers use good technique; it's as simple as that. If you tend to hit skulls and/or chunks from just off the green, chances are your technique could use a brush up. For starters, try moving the ball back in your stance and keeping your feet close together. Next, keep the weight on your front foot and start your hands and grip in front of your forward leg.

Now you have a great chance of hitting a solid shot because you are set up to make a descending blow on the ball, hitting the ground and the ball at the same time.

Most great chippers also employ an open stance in order to help them turn through the shot easier. Remember, just as in putting, you want to keep your wrists quiet (little or no hinging) and your hands soft (so don't squeeze the rubber off your grip).

One other helpful hint: avoid whipping the club quickly inside the target line on the take-away. Taking the club straight back will ensure solid contact.

Chipping:
During the stroke, a key thought is turning your chest to the target and keeping your hands quiet.

Bunker Play

An abundance of students looking for help are poor bunker players. The main reason is that they have never spent any quality time in a practice bunker.

Proper technique helps, but there's nothing like practice in this case, and a lot of it, to build confidence in a bunker.

Most professionals practice bunker shots every week while on tour in order to stay sharp. If a touring pro needs that much practice, why should an amateur player think he or she needs less?

"You may not know it, but Mike Weir is one of the best bunker players I've ever seen," Mike Wilson said. "Not only is his technique solid, but he exudes confidence over every bunker shot. I think he enjoys the challenge and, better yet, enjoys practicing."

Bunker Shot Set-up:
For bunker shots, ensure that the ball is played forward in the stance with an open clubface (1). Also make sure the club is kept open in the backswing (2). This makes the bounce of the sand wedge work correctly.

Weir's fundamentals are consistently good. First, he has a wide, athletic and open stance. Second, he grips the club with the face open, and third, he plays the ball forward in his stance. These set-up keys allow him to use the bounce of his wedge properly, giving him a great amount of control over the ball. A follow-through is also imperative. The sand wedge should never end up stuck in the sand. Following through with the wedge face open, or pointed to the sky, as long as possible also helps to use the bounce of the wedge. This is also what helps Weir hit such high, soft bunker shots and it creates maximum backspin.

The next time you are at a PGA Tour event, take the time to watch Mike in a bunker, either at the practice range or during his round. You are likely to be impressed by his technique.

Bunker Shots:
With a steady body position (2), (3), the wedge touches the sand just behind the ball and the follow-through helps to splash it out. As with a pitch shot, turning the chest to the target is imperative, as is keeping your feet dug into the sand

Putting

"As a teaching professional, I am always amazed at the small number of requests I get each year for putting lessons," Mike Wilson said. "If you think about it, there is an 18-shot variable between one- and two-putting every hole in a round of golf. Eighteen shots is a large variable on your score, and that's not even considering the wasted number of strokes from three- and four-putts."

Putting Set-up:
First, determine a good putting posture by standing square to the line of putt, bending from the hips and letting the arms fall in front of you. Weir uses a small, soft, soccer-style ball to help him find the right posture (1) and from there, with his eyes directly over the ball, slips his hands on his putter for the set-up (2).

Putting Drill:
Keeping the small, soft soccer-style ball between the elbows promotes a one-piece motion (2), (3) of the shoulders, arms, hands and putter.

If that perspective about play on the greens isn't enough to inspire you to practice your putting, what is?

In the 2000 Memorial Tournament, Weir needed only 22 putts during his Friday round. He putted brilliantly, finishing first in the putting statistics kept by the PGA Tour for that event. Mike is a wonderful putter, one of the best in the world. Here are some keys he uses that are bound to help you.

As with your swing, good putting starts with a good set-up position. Try to make a square stance and align your shoulders parallel to your putting line as well. Next, bend forward from your hips but keep the weight on your heels. You will feel your arms hanging from your shoulders at this point. Now, just bring your palms together in front of you and press them together. Keep pressing your palms together and bring your hands slightly toward your chest by bending your elbows.

Now you are in wonderful position to practice the correct feeling of the stroke.

The putting swing or stroke is to be controlled by the shoulders and muscles of the upper back. Try to not move your legs or hips during putts, and keep your wrists as quiet as possible. This type of stroke will produce a very consistent roll and feel.

The putting grip that most pros use is called the reverse overlap. For a left-handed player, this means placing the right index finger on the outside of the left pinky finger. This connects the hands to help them work as one piece. In general, the putter grip itself should be held more in the palms and less in the fingers, but remember, this is generally the case only with a putter. This promotes a one-piece action that eliminates any inclination to flip the wrists or use the hands for power. Good putters will also keep a light touch on their putter, in order to heighten their awareness of the distance to the hole and the speed of a putt.

A great drill for learning feel and touch is to hit a few putts one-handed. First, try it with one hand and then the other. Start by hitting a few putts four feet, and then move back two feet for a few more, and so on. Keep the rhythm smooth and controlled. A good putting stroke is never jerky. Just let the club swing and don't force it. Weir also likes to place tees in the putting green and putt to them to work on his distance control.

Putting Drill:
To help with touch and distance control, Weir likes to place
tees on the putting green about 3, 6 and 9 feet away. Using
three balls, he putts to each tee in succession starting with
the farthest one. To successfully complete the drill, make
one ball stop beside each tee.

Creating Backspin

One of the seemingly great mysteries of the game is how the pros create so much backspin on their approach shots. You have no doubt seen a television broadcast where a pro hits the green and the ball bounces forward, then spins back quickly. This is the result of solid contact and a clean hit on the ball. It is also caused by the player hitting down on the ball instead of trying to scoop it up into the air.

This downward strike actually traps the ball between the face of the club and the ground and then the ball rolls up the face as it goes through impact.

This rolling action, which is very subtle and can't be felt, occurs through impact when a player's swing is working correctly. If you hook the ball a lot or hit the ball low, chances are that you have never really experienced a lot of backspin.

This is because the face of the club is probably fairly closed during your swing. If this is the case, have someone help you with your grip. Chances are it's a little too strong.

In order to create backspin, you must be willing to create a divot. Many students are simply unwilling to hit the ground. It may be fear or it may be that a past experience has proven it to be painful. Whatever the reason, they avoid the ground like the plague.

The best way to practice spinning the ball is to hit bunker shots. Find a practice bunker and stay in there for a while. If you start with the face open and keep it open through impact, you will spin the ball quite easily. Just hit the sand first a couple of inches behind the ball and keep your hands quiet. In no time, you will see some backspin and at the same time, see your fear of hitting the ground disappear.

In-between Shots

In recent years, there has been much talk about how the art of shotmaking has been lost. It's not necessarily so. If you follow the PGA Tour consistently, as well as the highest amateur ranks, you know the golf world is still full of wonderful shot-makers.

A skill mastered by any of the true shotmakers is the half shot, a shot used to approach the green.

Backspin:
If spin is what you need on a wedge shot, then don't be afraid to make a divot (1). Hitting slightly down on the ball and following through without releasing the clubhead (3) will help you find the spin you need.

Half Shots:
By limiting the backswing to a controlled, less-than-full
take-away (1), taking a little distance off a shot becomes
much easier.

Many golfers can hit a full shot but taking a little distance off the shot
is usually a tall order. Mike Weir loves to hit little six-irons or eight-irons
instead of big sevens or nines. This is because he knows the value of keeping his swing and the ball under control. If you want to gear back a little
to gain some control, start by knowing the distances your clubs hit the ball
under normal conditions. This requires time on the practice tee.

Remember to make a purposeful downswing but keep the finish under control by limiting the distance your arms swing (2). Solid contact is much easier with this kind of controlled swing.

For the lower-handicap golfer, precision and accuracy are of the utmost importance. If you're trying to learn shotmaking with half shots, start by using one more club than normal. Second, use only a three-quarter backswing, and make a positive and purposeful downswing.

You're bound to find it's so much easier to control your shots when you're not trying to hit them with full force.

Conclusion

WELL, I HOPE you've learned a little bit more about me and picked up a few keys that will help your game. As you have read, having a basic understanding of the true fundamentals of the golf swing is the most reliable way to make positive change.

In my case, I'll always be in search of the most efficient swing possible so that I can become the best player I can be. The process is what I enjoy the most.

I've always been long-term goal-oriented – that translates to my swing goals as well. I'm not looking for quick fixes. As Nick Price has told me, you should try to improve your faults a little bit each year. Doing this will bring about true change in the long-run.

I have a better understanding now of what Nick was talking about. He's been a world-class player for a long time, but when he began to dominate the world of golf in 1991, and then with four wins in 1993 and five in 1994, it wasn't because of some dramatic, one-time change in his game. He worked hard at getting better every day for quite some time and you obviously can see how he was rewarded for that work.

You've read about some of the changes I've made in my game. Working at those changes little by little is very important. It's something that any golfer can do, and something that will help you to strike the ball more solidly on a more consistent basis.

And that makes the game a whole lot more fun.

Glossary

Around the Corner
Instead of the clubhead going straight back during the take-away, it is moved quickly inside the proper path by the hands and arms. The clubhead winds up going around a left-hander's left leg and behind the body.

Bounce
The rounded, bottom side of most sand wedges that keeps the clubhead from digging into the sand.

Closed Face or Shut Position
This occurs when the clubface at address has a hooded look and, for a left-hander, is aimed to the right of the target. At the top of the backswing, the face of a club with a closed face will point toward the sky.

Forward Press
At address, before the start of the take-away, a small move by the hands that puts the hands or the handle of the club ahead of the ball.

Hinge
A term referring to a simple wrist cock, or the degree of wrist cock during the swing.

Open Face
This occurs at address when the club face has a toe-back look and the leading edge of the face is aimed, for a left-hander, to the left of the target. At the top of the backswing, the face of the club with an open face will point toward the ground.

Open Shoulders

Where a line extending from the shoulders points to the right of a left-hander's target. This line can be easily determined by placing the shaft of any club against both shoulders across the upper chest.

Quiet Hands

Also known as passive hands, refers to limiting excessive hand movement during impact. A player shouldn't be trying to direct the ball with his hands or wrists as he comes into contact with it.

Square Face

This occurs at any time during the swing when the leading edge of the club is in the same position as a left-hander's right forearm. At address, a square face points at the target, of course. At the top of the backswing, a square face mirrors the forearm and is approximately at a 45-degree angle to the ground. To keep the face square, the wrists and hands must not change the position of the club face in the take-away.

Career Highlights

IKE WEIR has had many accomplishments throughout his career. This summary of Mike's top 25 finishes and other significant events from 1997 through to the end of the 2000 season makes it easy to track his progress.

1997

Date	Tournament	Position	Total Score		Official Money
06/08	B.C. Tel Pacific Open	1	271	-13	$22,000 (Cdn)
07/27	Canadian Masters	1	266	-18	$36,000 (Cdn)
08/10	CPGA Championship	P2	276	-8	$12,500 (Cdn)
12/08	PGA Tour Qualifying Tournament	T26	422	-7	$ 6,000 (US)

1998

Date	Tournament	Position	Total Score		Official Money
2/15	*United Airlines Hawaiian Open	T21	273	-15	$ 18,000 (US)
4/05	*Freeport-McDermott Classic	T19	284	-4	$ 18,487 (US)
8/23	*Sprint International	T21			$ 20,800 (US)
8/30	*Greater Vancouver Open	T5	273	-11	$ 65,500 (US)
9/20	*B.C. Open	T7	279	-9	$ 48,375 (US)
11/23	PGA Tour Qualifying Tournament	1	408	-24	$ 50,000 (US)

* PGA Tour official event tournament; P2 means lost in play-off; T means tied.

1999

....

Date	Tournament	Position	Total Score		Official Money
1/31	*Phoenix Open	T22	286	+2	$ 30,000 (US)
2/28	*Touchstone Energy Tucson Open	T13	280	-8	$ 47,143 (US)
4/04	*BellSouth Classic	T5	274	-14	$ 95,000 (US)
4/18	*MCI Classic	T10	278	-6	$ 65,000 (US)
4/25	*Greater Greensboro Chrysler Classic	T25	283	-5	$ 19,847 (US)
6/06	*Memorial Tournament	T24	285	-3	$ 20,181 (US)
6/29	Export 'A' Canadian Skins Game	1			$ 210,000 (Cdn)
7/04	*Motorola Western Open	2	276	-12	$ 270,000 (US)
8/15	*PGA Championship	T10	285	-3	$ 72,166 (US)
9/05	*Air Canada Championship	1	266	-18	$ 450,000 (US)
9/19	B.C. Open	T10	278	-10	$ 41,600 (US)
10/10	*Michelob Championship at Kingsmill	3	275	-9	$ 170,000 (US)
10/17	*Las Vegas Invitational	T19	346	-14	$ 32,500 (US)

* PGA Tour official event tournament; P2 means lost in play-off; T means tied.

2000

....

Date	Tournament	Position	Total Score		Official Money
1/09	*Mercedes Championships	T4	285	-7	$ 127,500 (US)
1/30	*Phoenix Open	T10	274	-10	$ 66,400 (US)
2/06	*AT&T Pebble Beach National Pro-Am	T7	278	-10	$ 120,500 (US)
2/27	*WGC-Andersen Consulting Match Play	T17			$ 50,000 (US)
3/12	*Honda Classic	T19	276	-12	$ 30,514 (US)
3/19	*Bay Hill Invitational	T7	279	-9	$ 96,750 (US)
5/21	*MasterCard Invitational	T8	274	-6	$ 89,100 (US)
5/28	*Memorial Tournament	4	276	-12	$ 148,800 (US)
6/11	*Buick Classic	T19	284	E	$ 36,360 (US)
6/18	*U.S. Open	T16	293	+9	$ 65,214 (US)
8/06	*The International Presented by Qwest	T19			$ 47,250 (US)
8/24	*WGC-NEC Invitational	T24	283	+3	$ 52,333 (US)
10/08	*Michelob Championship at Kingsmill	P2	271	-13	$ 324,000 (US)
10/15	*Invensys Classic at Las Vegas	T12	337	-23	$ 89,250 (US)
11/05	*The Tour Championship	21	282	+2	$ 94,000 (US)
11/12	*WGC-American Express Championship	1	277	-11	$1,000,000 (US)
12/10	WGC-EMC World Cup	T10	271		$ 28,750 (US)

* PGA Tour official event tournament; P2 means lost in play-off; T means tied.

2001

············

Date	Tournament	Position	Total Score		Official Money
1/14	*Mercedes Championships	T12	281	-11	$78,000(US)
1/28	*Phoenix Open	T23	278	-6	$31,400(US)
2/04	*AT&T Pebble Beach National Pro Am	T8	278	-10	$112,000(US)
2/11	*Buick Invitational	T5	272	-16	$133,000(US)
3/04	*Genuity Championship	2	272	-16	$486,000(US)
4/01	*BellSouth Classic	2	283	-5	$356,400(US)
5/13	*Verizon Byron Nelson Classic	T11	269	-11	$78,955(US)
6/17	*U.S. Open Championship	T19	285	+5	$63,426(US)
7/08	*Advil Western Open	T3	275	-13	$208,800(US)
8/19	*PGA Championship	T16	277	-3	$70,667(US)
8/26	*WGC-NEC Invitational	25	283	+3	$53,000(US)
10/07	*Michelob Championship at Kingsmill	T12	277	-7	$73,500(US)
11/04	*THE TOUR Championship	P1	270	-14	$900,000(US)
11/18	WGC-EMC World Cup	T6	268	-20	$47,500(US)

* PGA Tour official event; P1 means won in play-off; T means tied.

2002

Date	Tournament	Position	Total Score		Official Money
1/06	*Mercedes Championships	T14	284	-8	$83,500(US)
2/24	*WGC-Accenture Match Play Championship	T17			$55,000(US)
3/03	*Genuity Championship	T16	284	-4	$63,802(US)
3/10	*The Honda Classic	T11	275	-13	$63,350(US)
3/24	*THE PLAYERS Championship	T19	288	E	$78,000(US)
4/07	*BellSouth Classic	T17	283	-5	$57,000(US)
4/14	*Masters Tournament	T24	290	+2	$46,480(US)
6/09	*Buick Classic	T12	279	-5	$66,500(US)
8/25	*WGC-NEC Invitational	T24	282	-2	$45,000(US)
9/08	*Bell Canadian Open	T22	279	-9	$37,133(US)
9/22	*WGC-American Express Championship	T15	274	-14	$65,000(US)
12/15	WGC-EMC World Cup	T8	261	-27	$37,500(US)

* PGA Tour official event; T means tied.

2003

....

Date	Tournament	Position	Total Score		Official Money
1/26	*Phoenix Open	T9	267	-17	$112,00(US)
2/02	*Bob Hope Chrysler Classic	1	330	-30	$810,000(US)
2/09	*AT&T Pebble Beach National Pro Am	T3	276	-12	$290,000(US)
2/23	*Nissan Open	P1	275	-9	$810,000(US)
3/02	*WGC-Accenture Match Play Championship	T17			$60,000(US)
3/09	*Ford Championship at Doral	T14	278	-10	$77,500(US)
4/13	Masters Tournament	P1	281	-7	$1,080,000(US)

* PGA Tour official event; P1 means won in play-off; T means tied.

Index

Tim Campbell

Tim Campbell is a golf writer at the *Winnipeg Free Press*, *Score* magazine and other golf publications. The allure of the game didn't present itself to Tim until his first lesson at the age of 12, a session he and brother Chris reluctantly attended, but the seed grew to an ever-increasing attraction and enthusiasm a short time later. A left-handed player himself, Tim's ongoing fascination is with the mental side of the game and trying to shave a shot or two off his single-digit handicap. Originally from the Guelph and Kitchener, Ontario area, Tim now makes his home in Winnipeg.

Scott Morrison

Scott Morrison is the sports editor of *The Toronto Sun* and a hockey analyst on CTV Sportsnet. He also enjoys the game of golf and hits from the left side. Scott's previous books have focused in the area of hockey. *The Days Canada Stood Still* focused on the 1972 Canada-Russia hockey series, while *Fire on Ice* was about great international series. His most recent title was a best seller about Wayne Gretzky, entitled *The Great One*. Scott lives in Toronto with his wife Kathy and their son Mark.

Mike Wilson

PGA professional Mike Wilson became hooked on golf at the age of 15 when he began working at a popular public course in Albuquerque, New Mexico. His passion for the game grew and led him to full-time coaching positions. He is now teaching under his own name in Palm Desert, California. Wilson was introduced to Mike Weir by a mutual friend and golf professional in 1996. They have since embarked on a long-term plan, along with sport psychologist, Dr. Rich Gordin, to help Weir improve all facets of his game.

Mike Wilson can be contacted at the Academy at Desert Willow at (760) 340-4057 or via email at mwilson@golfhound.com.

Rich Gordin

Dr. Rich Gordin is a professor at Utah State University in Logan, Utah. He has been consulting with Olympic and professional athletes for 25 years. Dr. Gordin was the team sport psychologist for the USA Women's Gymnastics Team in Seoul in 1988. He is currently working with the USA Track and Field Team and many PGA Touring professionals. He has published extensively in the area of performance enhancement. Dr. Gordin began working with Mike Weir and coach Mike Wilson in 1997.